For the Love of Learning

Information and Resources for Combining Charlotte Mason and Classical Education

Jenny Sockey

xulon
PRESS

Library of Congress Control Number: 2002106167
ISBN 1-591601-21-5

Unless otherwise indicated, Bible quotations are taken from the New King James Version.

Xulon Press
11350 Random Hills Road
Suite 800
Fairfax, VA 22030
(703) 279-6511
XulonPress.com

To order additional copies, call 1-866-909-BOOK (2665).

Table of Contents

Dedication

I would like to dedicate this book to my heavenly Father to whom I owe my all, my whole being, to Jesus Christ his only Son and my Saviour, and the Holy Spirit who gave life to my words.

I would also like to acknowledge all the wonderful people that I took from their wisdom and made quotes from.

Addison, The Spectator
C. S. Lewis
Catherine Levison
Charlotte Mason
Clifton Fadiman
Dorothy L. Sayers
Doug Wilson
Dr. Francis Schaeffer
E. Kitching
Encyclopedia Brittanica on the History of Education
Erasmus
Escondido Tutorial Service, Classical Christian
    Homeschooling
Foundations Academy, A Parent's Primer
Fritz Hinrichs, Classical Worldview
George MacDonald
Gladys Hunt
Isaiah, NKJ
J.P. Inman
James V. Schall
Jesse Wise & Susan Wise Bauer

Karen Andreola
Laura Berquist
Leo Strauss
Mary Lynch
Mortimer J. Aider
Otto Willmann
Peattie
Public Charter Schools & Core Knowledge Movement,
    The Lexington Institute
Robert A. Heinlein
Robert Hutchins
Sister Wendy Beckett
Susan Schaeffer MacAulay
Terry W. Glaspey
William H. Willimon
William Makepeace Thackeray

And lastly but not at all least I would lke to thank Maggie rayner for a fabulous laying out of my book, thank you so much, may God richly bless you and your family.

Introduction

I have four children, all grown now, and five grandchildren with #6 on the way. I started homeschooling in 1981. I am presently a respite foster mother of disabled children. I started a homeschool used-book store to help local homeschooling moms stretch their budgets and to encourage the recycling of good used curriculum. My bookstore, *Homeschool Potpourri*, is the oldest of its kind. It became the largest homeschool used-book store in the United States. Through the operation of the bookstore, I have met and talked to thousands of homeschooling parents all across the nation. I have heard from parents using every different method of homeschooling imaginable. This book is borne out of those discussions and my personal experience.

For years, I had books by and about Charlotte Mason on my shelves. Although I am a voracious reader, these volumes stood unread by me for many years. My own children were almost grown when I finally made a serious study of Charlotte Mason. Once I started, I began to read everything I could get my hands on about her method and life. About this time, I began to hear people talk about another method, the *Classical Education* approach. As I listened, it sounded wonderful, so I began to search out information of this style of teaching. Although the methods themselves are dissimilar, they are dissimilar in such a way that they can be lovingly combined. The classical method concentrates much more on the "what" and "when" of teaching, while the Charlotte Mason approach emphasizes the "how".

I combined the Charlotte Mason and classical methods

for the last few years that I homeschooled my own children. I also ran a small school from my home, and continued this combined approach. It was truly the best of both worlds. It worked so well that I have become a Charlotte Mason-Classical Education advocate.

This book is not intended to be a comprehensive guide to either the Charlotte Mason or Classical Education method of teaching children. There are a lot of books pertaining to Charlotte Mason and Classical Education already. The purpose of this book is both to promote and support the combination of the Charlotte Mason and Classical Education models of education. This book will also provide a fairly comprehensive listing of resources suitable for this endeavor. I have listed materials, which I consider to be the "cream of the crop" from my own experience and through the many recommendations and requests at my bookstore. It is my hope and desire that this book will assist parents in the determination and location of resources, which fit both their Charlotte Mason and Classical Education philosophy and their children's unique needs and talents.

Part I— The Methods

CHARLOTTE MASON

"We parents can become quite anxious about covering and completing all the requirements for a particular grade level, and seeing that our children excel in the skills demanded of that grade level. It's a woeful business when parents look toward doing what the grand system of education says is right for a child within their little homeschool. But when parents pursue knowledge for its own sake they need not be subservient to this grand system. Many young children hunger for knowledge. Yet they dutifully serve the system of textbook overview with never-ending worksheets and, under a system that does not feed their hunger for vibrant, vital knowledge, they begin to pine away.

"It is then that Mother loses confidence and feels discouraged and unqualified to teach. The children, for their part, find it harder and harder to obey. Parents and children alike are stuck in a system that stifles curiosity and initiative, and makes learning uninteresting."

Karen Andreola,
A Charlotte Mason Companion, page 29

Charlotte Mason is known as the "Mother of Homeschooling." She was a devout Christian who loved children. Charlotte spent her whole life either teaching children or teaching young women how to be governesses and to teach using her philosophy. She was born in England in 1842, and was educated by her parents at home (homeschooled). Charlotte was suddenly orphaned at the age of 16. She loved and valued children so highly that she never married, but continued teaching all of her life. Charlotte Mason lived into her eighties and died on January 16, 1923 in her sleep.

Charlotte Mason founded her "House of Education" in Ambleside in 1892. She had four students in her first year. By her third year, she had thirteen. In 1880, she wrote a series of geography books that were quite well received. However, her book, *Home Education*, proved to be even more popular. Soon after this, the *Parents National Education Union* was formed. By 1890, the Union had its own magazine, *The Parents Review*. This magazine was done by Charlotte herself. The magazine continued to be published long after Charlotte's death. Charlotte wrote five more books during her lifetime, which have been reproduced as a six-volume set by Charlotte Mason Research and Supply Company.

A Brief Overview of the Charlotte Mason Method

This overview is very short and does not really do justice to Charlotte Mason. It is included here only for those who know very little about her life and work. It is by no means meant to replace the volumes written about Charlotte, or, for that matter, those she wrote herself. Please refer to the resources listed at the end of this section for more in-depth information on, and by, Charlotte Mason.

Homeschooling parents today may take many of Charlotte Mason's teaching principles for granted. But for her time, Charlotte was a pioneer. She was a children's advocate long before the term was coined. Her teaching style was child-sensitive and gentle. She coaxed the extraordinary out of her pupils while other teachers of her day were "stuffing" children with learning as one might stuff a feather pillow. Below are some of the cornerstones of Charlotte's home education philosophy:

- Living Books & Whole Books
- Best Minds
- Narration
- Nature Study
- Short Lessons
- No Homework before Thirteen
- Atmosphere, Discipline, Life
- Good Habits
- The Science of Relations

Living Books and Whole Books

Charlotte Mason believed that children should not be treated "like children." Children shouldn't be taught as though they aren't old enough to think about or appreciate the finer things in life. In fact, Charlotte was very opposed to offering children the "simplified" versions of books or texts, especially the ones that had endless questions at the end of every chapter. ("Why not let children come up with their own questions?" she would ask.) She found most text-books dull and insipid, and was sure that children found them dull and insipid as well. She called these books "twaddle."

> *"A child has not begun his education until he has acquired the habit of reading to himself, with interest and pleasure, books fully on a level with his intelligence. I am speaking now of his lesson-books, which are all too apt to be written in a style of insufferable twaddle, probably because they are written by persons who have never chanced to meet a child. All who know children know that they do not talk twaddle and do not like it, and prefer that which appeals to their under-*

standing. Their lesson-books should offer matter for their reading, whether aloud or to themselves; therefore, they should be written with literary power. As for the matter of these books, let us remember that children can take in ideas and principles, whether the latter be moral or mechanical, as quickly and clearly as we do ourselves (perhaps more so); but detailed processes, lists and summaries, blunt the edge of a child's delicate mind. Therefore, the selection of their first lesson books is a matter of grave importance, because it rests with these to give children the idea that knowledge is supremely attractive and that reading is delightful. Once the habit of reading his lesson-books with delight is set up in a child, his education is not completed, but ensured; he will go on for himself in spite of the obstructions which schools too commonly throw in his way."

Charlotte Mason,
Home Education, pp229

"I came late to a love for books. Like most children of my generation, I spent countless hours in front of the television set, eyes glued to its latest offerings. Arriving home from school, I would throw my coat and lunch box onto the couch and flip on the television set, always somewhat amazed as that hard little star of white light whined and then exploded into a chaos of colours that magically oriented themselves into a viewable picture. It was a miracle, all these shows available with the flick of a switch. In the evenings after dinner I would bask in the flickering blue

light of the TV, my elbows on the floor, my legs sprawled out behind me. I was not a particularly discerning viewer, but I watched with childlike concentration whatever happened to be on at the time: "Gilligan's Island," "The Brady Bunch," "The Flintstones," "Wild, Wild West." Now the very mentions of these programs evokes a wave of wistful (if slightly embarrassed) nostalgia. Though the TV was a great way to fill my time, the hours spent in front of it always left me somewhat empty. What was missing, I think, was a sense of wonder. I was to find that this need would best be met by books."

Terry W. Glaspey

Charlotte Mason said, "The finding of this power," which is described as, "sensing a passage, is as the striking of a vein of gold in that fabulously rich country, human nature." Charlotte also said, "The best thought the world possesses is stored in books; we must open books to children, the best books; our own concern is abundant provision and orderly serving." J.P. Inman describes Charlotte's philosophy regarding books,

"She was a great believer in big books. Great literature speaks for itself and an author is his own best expounder. The poet and the writer can speak directly to the soul of the child. What can not be understood directly can well wait for another time. A great author writes not that he may be expounded, but that he may ring a bell in the secret chambers of the heart."

Living Books. Living Books are books that "come alive" when you read them. They are usually books about real people and real things, but may include "historical fiction" and similar types of books. Dull, boring or silly books that talk down to a child "blunt the edge of a child's delicate mind"! But living books are interesting. They come alive with information and characters. They are filled with real lives and real dramas: people getting married, having children, dealing with illness or hardships. Living books excite you about the subject, transport you back in time, or evoke the emotions of the characters in your heart. Charlotte Mason said of living books that they are "clothed in literary language"

> *"The familiar faces of my books welcomed me. I threw myself into my reading chair and gazed around me with pleasure. All my old friends present — there in spirit, ready to talk with me any moment when I was in the mood, making no claim upon my attention when I was not."*
>
> George MacDonald

Whole Books. There are two types of "whole" books. Any book written on a single topic by a single author is a whole book. Many times, the subject in a whole book is "the love of the author's life." (We can usually assume that an author has some passion for a subject to which he devotes an entire book.) This "love" is generally evident throughout the book by virtue of the care and interest given the subject. Textbooks, which often only provide a glimpse of a particular subject, tend to be dry and boring. A whole book is bound to be more interesting than a textbook due to the author's knowledge, experience and passion.

The second type of "whole" book is an unabridged (unaltered) version of a book. This refers to classic works of literature, novels, plays or poetry. Textbooks or abridged versions may include a chapter, or a condensed or simplified version of a story. This dilutes both the meaning and the passion of the author, and may result in a dull or dry translation. Apparently, textbooks and abridged versions of books were first implemented for use by the "lower classes" as it was believed that they could not handle "a whole" book.

Best Minds

Charlotte believed that a child's mind was fed on ideas.

"The life of the mind is sustained upon ideas"
Charlotte Mason

"For this reason, we owe it to every child to put him in communication with great minds, that he may get at great thoughts. With the minds, that is, of those who have left us great works. And the only vital method of education appears to be that children should read worthy books. Many worthy books."

Charlotte Mason,
A Philosophy of Education, 1925

Charlotte did not believe in "talking down" or "reading-down" to children. If one is going to read <u>Heidi</u>, she reasoned, they should read the author's original <u>Heidi</u>, not a watered-down "children's" version of it. It is precisely in the reading of the original works that children make contact with the "best minds." Erasmus, a Christian Scholar wrote,

"I have no patience with the stupidity of the average teacher of grammar who wastes precious years in hammering rules into children's heads. For it is not by learning rules that we acquire the

*power of speaking a language, but by daily inter-
course with those accustomed to express themselves with exactness and refinement, and by the
copious reading of the best authors."*

The Treatise of Erasmus, De Ratione Studii
(Upon the Right Method of Instruction), 1511

Narration

Narration is the process of re-telling something in one's
own words. Charlotte found that the use of narration made
children more attentive. (Each child listening to a story is
aware that he might be asked to re-tell it.)

> *"As knowledge is not assimilated until it is repro-
> duced, children should 'tell back' after a single
> reading or hearing; or should write on some part
> of what they have read."*

Charlotte Mason,
A Philosophy of Education, 1925

Through the process of re-telling, a teacher can easily
determine if a child has understood what has been taught.
More important, Charlotte realized that other methods of
testing comprehension (questions at the end of the chapter,
tests) spotlight the areas that a child *does not know.*
Narration, on the other hand, highlights what a child *does
know.* Therefore, she reasoned, narration promotes success
rather than failure. Narration allows a child the freedom to
discuss what he has learned, not necessarily what a teacher
or a textbook tells him that he ought to have learned.

> *"Children benefit from working steadily through a
> well-chosen book. And if they narrate it to you, it*

> *will become theirs. But more happens. Because*
> *they've tackled a complete book, they become*
> *acquainted with its flow and its use of language.*
> *They are students of another person— the author."*
>
> Susan Schaeffer MacAulay,
> *For the Children's Sake*, 1984

Nature Study

The study of nature is particularly helpful in the development of the power of observation. Charlotte felt that children were also happier and healthier when given the opportunity to spend time in natural settings. She took her children on long walks, in all kinds of weather.

She believed that children should be able to identify all of the natural elements around them—from shrubs and trees to birds and other creatures. She taught children about geology and geography, field crops, and constellations. The children were given high-quality sketchpads and art supplies, and were encouraged to record their observations in the form of pictures and journal entries.

Short Lessons

Charlotte believed that it is the duty of the teacher to capture the attention of the child. She suggested that it is up to the teacher to form the necessary habit of attention in the child, and also to present material to the child that is worthy of his interest. With the focus of the mind on a subject so directed, Charlotte reasoned, lessons could be short and still be effective. Difficult subjects, such as math, might take up to 20 minutes for elementary-aged children, whereas simpler subjects would take even less time. Charlotte's system of short lessons allowed many subjects and much variety to be presented in a day, resulting in a more interesting and complete education.

No Homework Before Thirteen

Charlotte did not assign homework to children under the age of thirteen.

> *"Another attraction of Charlotte's philosophy is that her schools never gave homework to students under the age of thirteen. When a child follows her method, there is no need for homework in the elementary years, because the child immediately deals with the literature at hand and proves his mastery by narrating at the time of the reading. Studies have proved homework to be less effective than this form of immediate reinforcement."*
>
> Karen Andreola,
> *A Charlotte Mason Companion,* 1998

Atmosphere, Discipline, Life

> *"Education is an atmosphere, a discipline, a life."*
>
> Charlotte Mason

> *"Education is a life; that life is sustained on ideas; ideas are of spiritual origin, and that we get them chiefly as we convey them to one another. The duty of parents is to sustain a child's inner life with ideas as they sustain his body with food."*
>
> Charlotte Mason, *Volume 2,* pp 39

Charlotte believed in a "liberal education" for everyone, including girls. Liberal, in this sense, means "wide". A liberal education is one in which children are given a broad base of knowledge, learning as much as possible about each subject. Students in Charlotte Mason's school were given lessons on the Bible, government, history, math, geography, science, anatomy, vocabulary, nature, art, and poetry. They studied three foreign languages (Latin, French and German), and the works of people like Shakespeare and Homer.

Charlotte felt that a liberal education was necessary in order for children to grow up to be complete citizens, knowledgeable in many things, able to converse on many topics, and aware of how their particular occupation (their specialization of education) fit in with all the other occupations of the world. Her focus was to encourage a child's natural love of learning, and to resist any book or method, which would discourage this natural impulse. Schooling in the home was ideal. Home education offered the comfort and flexibility that was so central to Charlotte's methods.

> *"We have a definite mission — to bring fullness of life to the children. It is more possible to carry out this mission in a home schoolroom."*
>
> E. Kitching, *Parents Review* article, 1935

She also believed that education went far beyond studying. Charlotte asserted that the development of character is simply one part of a complete education. According to Charlotte, education deals...

> *"...curatively and methodically with every flaw in character... Discipline is not a punishment."*
>
> Charlotte Mason, Vol 1, pp 15

In 1891, she adopted the motto, "I am, I can, I ought, I will."

"Every child can say 'I am,'" said Charlotte, "because they are a child of God; a gift to their parents." They can say, "I can" because they have the power God has given to them to do a thing. "I ought" is the acknowledgement of duty, and "I will" is the decision to do what is right, not necessarily what is wanted.

Charlotte also believed that children are born "persons". She felt that a child's mind was born capable of great things. She said that one should "teach the child, not the textbook." Her emphasis was on a child's ability to learn, not a textbook's ability to teach. Conversely, many of the teachers of her day believed that only a rigorous education could produce a great mind, and that few minds could become great minds.

> *If we have not proved that a child is born a person with a mind as complete and as beautiful as his beautiful little body, we can at least show that he always has all the mind he requires for his occasions: that is, that his mind is the instrument of his education and that his education does not produce his mind."*
>
> Charlotte Mason

Good Habits

> *"We sow a thought and reap an act; we sow an act and reap a habit; we sow a habit and reap a character; we sow a character and reap a destiny."*
>
> William Makepeace Thackeray

If we fail to ease life by laying down habits of right thinking and right acting, habits of wrong thinking and wrong acting fix themselves of their own accord."

Charlotte Mason,
A Philosophy of Education, 1925

According to Charlotte, children have one great short-coming — a weak will. Weak, in the sense that they are unable to do what they know they ought, or they are easily led astray. "Children are given to be idle, to tell fibs, and to dawdle." Charlotte noted.

A child needs help to strengthen his own will. Charlotte believed that only one habit should be corrected at any given time, and that the process should take about six weeks. Her basic approach was that one should reason with the child at length about a particular habit needing improvement. It is vital that the child agrees, and even desires, to make a change. From this moment, there should be no further discussion. Should there be a lapse, Charlotte suggested using only a "look" or a light touch to remind the child of his commitment.

"Every effort of obedience which does not give him a sense of conquest over his own inclinations helps to enslave him. Instead, we want to invite his cooperation, let him heartily intend and purpose to do the thing he is bidden, and then it is his own will compelling him and not yours. He has begun the greatest effort, the highest accomplishment of human life, the making and the compelling of himself."

Charlotte Mason

According to Charlotte, a habit is "a mere automatic or

machine-like action with which conscious thought has nothing to do."

> *"Every day, every hour, the parents are either actively or passively forming those habits in their children, upon which, more than anything else, future character and conduct depend."*
>
> Charlotte Mason

Charlotte believed that habits begin as thoughts, "Thoughts defile a man; and thoughts purify a man." Therefore, it was of the utmost importance to develop good habits at an early age.

> *"Because, once certain mental habitudes are set up, their nature is to go on forever, unless they should be displaced by other habits."*

The idea that bad habits should be overlooked because children are "too young" or will "grow out" of them is in opposition to Charlotte's philosophy. She emphasized the importance of developing right habits, so that these habits would be automatic, especially in times of trial or emergency:

> *"In every sudden difficulty and temptation that requires an act of will, conduct is still apt to run on the lines of familiar habit."*
>
> Charlotte Mason

In terms of education, the habit of attention is vital.

> *"No intellectual habit is so important as that of attention: it is a mere habit but it is also the hallmark of an educated person."*
>
> Charlotte Mason, *A Philosophy of Education*, 1925

Attention, according to Charlotte, is the focus of mind brought to bear on a person or subject. Great minds have great focus. They are owned by experts in their field, or by counselors in whom one feels comfortable confiding. An unfocused mind is preoccupied with itself or it's surroundings, and cannot bring it's whole self to bear on a matter.

> *"Our generation is prone to amuse itself with fragmentary information and resources. We flip on the TV for brief programs, and then we think we know about the subjects they dealt with. A few paragraphs in a magazine, and we have formed an opinion. What is happening so often is that we are merely forming a habit of amusing our interest, and then forgetting the fragments. This is not education."*
>
> Susan Schaeffer MacAulay,
> *For the Children's Sake,* 1984

Science of Relations

> *"The idea that vivifies teaching... is that `Education is a Science of Relations'; by which phrase we mean that children come into the world with a natural [appetite] for, and affinity with, all the material of knowledge; for interest in the heroic past and in the age of myths; for a desire to know about everything that moves and lives; about strange places and strange peoples; for a wish to handle material and to make; a desire to run and ride and row and do whatever the law of gravitation permits.*
>
> *"Therefore... we endeavor that he shall have relations of pleasure and intimacy established with as*

many possible of the interests proper to him; not learning a slight or incomplete smattering about this or that subject, but plunging into vital knowledge, with a great field before him which in all his life he will not be able to explore. In this conception we get that 'touch of emotion' which vivifies knowledge, for it is probably that we feel only as we are brought into our proper vital relations."

Charlotte Mason

Charlotte felt that an understanding of all subjects was vital to the understanding of any. Art, literature, science and music must all be studied in relation to geography, culture, language and religion. Anything less might rob a child of the "wide outlook" so necessary to becoming well educated.

"A child should be brought up to have relations of force with earth and water, should run and ride, swim and skate, lift and carry; should know texture and work in material; should know by name, and where and how they live, at any rate, the things of the earth about him, its birds and beasts and creeping things, its herbs and trees; should be in touch with the literature, art and thought of the past and the present... He must have a living relationship with the present, its historic movement, its science, literature, art, social needs and aspirations.

"In fact, he must have a wide outlook, intimate relations all round; and force, virtue, must pass out of him, whether of hand, will or sympathy, wherever he touches. This is no impossible program. Indeed, it can be pretty well filled in by the time an intelligent boy or girl has reached the

age of thirteen or fourteen; for it depends, not
upon how much is learned, but upon how things
are learned."

Charlotte Mason, <u>Original Home Education Series</u>,
Vol 3, pp 161-162

Resources for More Information

A Charlotte Mason Companion, by Karen Andreola
A Charlotte Mason Education, by Catherine Levison
A Literary Education, by Catherine Levison
Charlotte Mason Study Guide, by Penny Gardner
Educating the Wholehearted Child, by Clay and Sally
    Clarkson
For the Children's Sake, by Susan Schaeffer MacAulay
For the Love of Reading, A How To Book, by Valerie
    Bendt
Language Arts... The Easy Way! by Cindy Rushton
More Charlotte Mason Education, by Catherine Levison
Nature Study... The Easy Way! by Cindy Rushton
Teaching Children, by Diane Lopez
The Original Homeschooling Series, (six-volume set) by
    Charlotte Mason
The Relaxed Home School, by Mary Hood, Ph. D.
Wild Days, by Karen Skidmore Rackliffe

CLASSICAL EDUCATION

*It has taken modern educators only 50 years to
disassemble an educational system that took
thousands of years to refine and establish. The
classical method was born in the ancient Greece*

and Rome and by the 16th century, it was used throughout the Western world. This system educated most of America's founding fathers as well as the world's philosophers, scientists and leaders between the 10th and 19th centuries. What other period can claim so many advances in science, philosophy, art, and literature?

Foundations Academy, *Understanding the Classical and Christian Difference—A Parent's Primer*

The Classical Education model was in widespread use until the mid-eighteen-hundreds. Wars, the Industrial Revolution, and the creation of huge public school "systems" began to influence the way people thought about education. For the first time, education began to be seen not so much as the "making of a man", but as the means to a vocational end. The ideal of *learning for learning's sake* was gradually replaced by the "expected outcomes" of our current society.

The modern educational goal is, in essence, to form a compliant citizen who will contribute economically and socially to his state. It is not necessarily detrimental to raise a child to fulfill these outcomes, but to do so without teaching him how to think, to search for truth and knowledge, and to learn to reason and grapple with great minds and great thoughts throughout history — that is a loss indeed.

method ↑ goal of classical ed.

"Classical Education produced Archimedes, St. Paul, St. Patrick and Columba, Dante, Leonardo Da Vinci, Galileo, Sir Isaac Newton, Christopher Columbus, Shakespeare, and our own great George Washington, Thomas Jefferson, and John Adams. These giants of their times are only the tip of the iceberg of the great philosophers, scientists, theologians, writers and artists that lived and

worked through the 18th century. They lived up to their potential, and each in their own way impacted the course of human history, because their potential was unlocked in part by Classical Education, which prepared them to grapple with the problems of their day."

Otto Willmann, *The Seven Liberal Arts*

"A good modern example of classical education...is C.S. Lewis. ...Lewis learned to translate French, Italian, German, Greek (especially Homer), carry on a rigorous line of reasoning and love fine literature."

Fritz Hinrichs, *Classical Worldview*

Advocates of Classical Education might argue that it is the "disassembly" of the traditional methods of education, which is directly responsible for the "disassembly" of society in general. Of the greatest importance to both Charlotte Mason and Classical educators was the relationship between all of the arts and sciences of man. It is when we teach history without faces, economy without geography, and science without morality that we wade out into deep waters.

"Classical Christian Education is further characterized by a rich exposure to the history, art, and culture of Western Civilization, including its languages (Latin and Greek), its philosophy and literature (the Great Books of Western Civilization and the Christian tradition), and the development of a Biblical worldview with Theology in its proper place as the Queen of the Sciences."

Foundations Academy, *Understanding the Classical and Christian Difference—A Parent's Primer*

Classical Education, like the Charlotte Mason method, is based on the "Liberal Arts" — the Latin *liberalis* meaning "suitable for freemen" and *arts* meaning "knowledge or skill". Hence, knowledge suitable for study by freemen, not slaves.

> *Beyond subject matter, classical education develops those skills that are essential in higher education and throughout life—- independent learning, critical thinking, and logical analysis.*
>
> Foundations Academy, *Understanding the Classical and Christian Difference—A Parent's Primer*

Classical Education is also based on the natural stages of intellectual development. Jesse Bauer, author of *A Well Trained Mind* wrote, "...the Classical theory of education, ...organizes learning around the maturing capacity of the child's mind." But, more importantly, it teaches a child how to think. Classical Education is not merely the accumulation of facts. In this book, the Classical Education method will be explored through the following topics:

- A "Liberal" Education
- The Trivium
- The Grammar (Poll-Parrot) Stage
- The Dialectic (Pert) Stage
- The Rhetoric (Poetic) Stage
- The Quadrivium
- The Subjects of Grammar, Logic & Rhetoric
- A Sense of "Mastery"

A "Liberal" Education

"Gram loquitur, Dia verba docet, Rhet verba colorat,
Mus canit, Ar numerat, Geo ponderat, Ast colit astra."

Which translated, means:
Grammar talks, Dialectic teaches words,
Rhetoric colors words, Music sings, Arithmetic numbers,
Geometry weighs, Astronomy tends the stars."

C. S. Lewis, *The Discarded Image*

The "Seven" original Liberal Arts were made up of two sets of study, the trivium, and the quadrivium. The trivium included the Grammar, Dialectic and Rhetoric stages. The quadrivium followed with Music, Arithmetic, Geometry and Astronomy.

A liberal, or broad, education assumes that one must be educated in many areas to become wholly educated (*Science of Relations*).

teach to the whole person

"Classical education aims to educate the "whole man" rather than produce specialists who are only capable in narrow areas of expertise"

Fritz Hinrichs, *Classical Worldview*

As Robert Hutchins puts it,

"Liberal arts is an end in itself... The aim of a liberal education is human excellence."

The Trivium

"In 1947, Dorothy Sayers articulated the educational concept of the trivium, an educational

model that had been used for centuries. When Douglas Wilson helped found Logos School in Moscow, Idaho during the 1980's, he revived this framework to bring about the rebirth of classical education. Presently, over 80 classical schools are operating in the U.S., most of which use the trivium to set their foundational educational philosophy.

"The trivium is simply a means of describing the learning stages of children as they mature. Parents often recognize the stages through which their children pass as they mature. The trivium focuses the educational method to best develop a knowledgeable, thinking, and articulate student. As the name implies, there are three stages represented in the trivium: Grammar, Logic, and Rhetoric."

Foundations Academy, *Understanding the Classical and Christian Difference—A Parent's Primer*

Tri is the Latin prefix for three, and *vium* (*via*), means "the way". The trivium, a three-fold method of instruction designed to match a child's developmental aptitudes and abilities, is central to the Classical Education method, but it is not the whole method.

The trivium advocates changes to the style and method of teaching as a child grows and increases in cognitive ability. The trivium does not refer to a list of subjects, but to the teaching of the *concrete*, the *analytical*, and the *abstract* of any given subject. These stages have also been defined as the stages of *knowledge, understanding,* and *wisdom.* Dorothy Sayers further defined the three stages as follows:

- Grammar: Mastery of the elements of a language
- Logic: Mastery of statements, definitions, arguments and fallacies
- Rhetoric: Mastery of creative and persuasive speech

The Grammar (Poll-Parrot) Stage

> *"Whom will He teach knowledge? And whom will He make to understand the message? Those just weaned from milk? Those just drawn from the breasts? For precept must be upon precept, precept upon precept, line upon line, line upon line, here a little, there a little."*
>
> Isaiah 28:9-10 NKJ

The grammar stage is designed to fill a child's head with knowledge. The early years should be dedicated to the memorization of facts, because it comes naturally, even enjoyably, to a child of this age to memorize and repeat. It does not matter that the facts are disjointed or scattered, only that a variety of sights, sounds and images accompany them, so as to fix them firmly in place for future use.

> *"During the Grammar phase, children are particularly adept at memorization. Young children learn songs, rhymes, and recite facts with relative ease. Because young children are so eager to memorize that they will make up non-sensical playground rhymes, we challenge them by providing substantial subject matter for them to memorize. Each subject has its own grammar.*
>
> *"In science, children memorize facts about nature. In math, children memorize times tables. In Latin,*

teachers emphasize vocabulary. Throughout each year in grammar school, classically educated children learn the factual foundation of each subject. We use songs, chants, and rhymes to help children enjoy the learning experience."

Foundations Academy, *Understanding the Classical and Christian Difference—A Parent's Primer*

Dorothy Sayers described the grammar stage the "Poll-parrot" stage:

The Poll-parrot stage is the one in which learning by heart is easy and, on the whole, pleasurable, whereas reasoning is difficult and, on the whole, little relished. At this age one readily memorizes the shapes and appearances of things; one likes to recite the number-plates of cars; one rejoices in the chanting of rhymes and the rumble and thunder of unintelligible polysyllables; one enjoys the mere accumulation of things.

"The Pert Age, which follows upon this (and, naturally, overlaps it to some extent) is only too familiar to all who have to do with children: it is characterized by contradicting, answering-back, liking to "catch people out" (especially one's elders) and the propounding of conundrums (especially the kind with a nasty verbal catch in them). Its nuisance-value is extremely high. It usually sets in about the Lower Fourth.

"The Poetic Age is popularly known as the "difficult" age. It is self-centered; it yearns to express itself; it rather specializes in being misunderstood; it is restless and tries to achieve indepen-

dence; and, with good luck and good guidance, it should show the beginnings of creativeness, a reaching-out towards a synthesis of what it already knows, and a deliberate eagerness to know and do some one thing in preference to all others. Now it seems to me that the lay-out of the Trivium adapts itself with a singular appropriateness to these three ages: Grammar to the Poll-parrot, Dialectic to the Pert, and Rhetoric to the Poetic age."

Dorothy L. Sayers, *The Lost Tools of Learning*

"The immature mind is more suited to absorption than argument. The critical and logical faculty simply doesn't develop until later on. The typical second-grader will take great joy in singing the latest television commercials to you word for word, but will stare at you slack-jawed if you ask him why the advertiser wants him to buy the product, or what the merits of the product are, or whether it's reasonably priced. There is nothing wrong with a child accumulating information that he doesn't yet understand. It all goes into the storehouse for use later on.

"Finally, there's the enjoyment factor. Children like lists at this age. They like rattling off rote information, even if they don't understand it. They enjoy the accomplishment, the look on the face of an adult when they trot out their stored knowledge, and the sounds of the syllables rolling off their tongues. As adults, we may tend to `protect' our children from memory work because we find it difficult and tedious. But most young children

enjoy repetition and delight in the familiarity of memorized words. How many times have you read Green Eggs and Ham to a four year old who already knows the entire book by heart?

"As your child's teacher, you'll serve as a source of information. In the early grades, you'll be telling your child stories, reading to him from history and science books, teaching him math facts. And you'll expect him to be able to repeat back to you the stories and facts he's heard. This process will train him to grasp facts and express them in his own words.

"Don't make k-4th students dig for information. Fill their mind and imagination with images and concepts, pictures and stories, spread knowledge out in front of them, and let them feast."

Jessie Wise & Susan Wise Bauer,
A Well Trained Mind

The Dialectic (Pert) Stage

"The Logic phase involves ordering facts into organized statements and arguments. During the middle school years, children are beginning to think independently. They often develop a propensity for argument. Classical education teaches children in this phase to argue well. The study of formal logic helps students understand the fundamentals of a good argument. Practice in making written and oral arguments helps to further develop these skills. Teachers encourage the use of argumentation in each subject.

"Again, each subject has its own logic. In science, we use the development and testing of hypothesis. In math, we develop students ability to logically orient numbers through the more abstract concepts of algebra and trigonometry."

Foundations Academy, *Understanding the Classical and Christian Difference—A Parent's Primer*

The Logic stage is also the stage where information is beginning to be processed. Connections are made between dates and events, history, music, art, inventions and culture. Imagine that the facts of the Grammar stage are groceries obtained from a store. They are all necessary, but random, and grouped inappropriately – canned goods with frozen foods, and vegetables beside laundry soap. It is the nature of the Logic-stage child to begin to see the disorder in his knowledge, and to question how it ought to look. The Logic-stage child begins to draw comparisons and, at the same time, find fault with real or imagined flaws in what he has been taught. This is the stage when a child begins to ask difficult questions, such as, "Should Christians fight in a war?" and "Why aren't there more doctors in Zimbabwe?"

"You'll concentrate on carrying on a dialogue with your child, a conversation in which you guide her toward the correct conclusions, while permitting her to find her own way. You'll allow the child to disagree with your conclusions, if she can support her points with the facts. And you'll expect her not simply to repeat what she's read, but to rework the material to reflect her own thoughts. Once she's done this, she'll have learned the material once and for all."

Jessie Wise & Susan Wise Bauer,
A Well Trained Mind

The Rhetoric (Poetic) Stage

"Rhetoric is the art of communicating well. Once a student has obtained a knowledge of the facts and developed the skills necessary to arrange those facts into arguments, he must develop the skill of communicating those arguments to others. During the high school years, students become concerned with what others think of them. Classical education helps students develop their minds to think and articulate concepts to others. Writing papers, researching, and orating ideas are skills required in all subjects."

Foundations Academy, *Understanding the Classical and Christian Difference—A Parent's Primer*

The Rhetoric stage is the high point of learning, and begins the process of mastery.

"Cognitively speaking, this stage is where abstract thought reaches its zenith. In this stage, the unknown can be explored because the known is understood; the hypothetical can be introduced and grasped with the mind. The mental jump can be made from the natural to the spiritual, from the practical to the theoretical. Self-expression finally comes into its own in the language arts; "hard" sciences and advanced mathematics are more easily mastered; history can be applied to economics and political science; and Bible study can turn to apologetics."

Escondido Tutorial Service, *Classical Christian Homeschooling*

Children in public schools receive little training in rhetoric. They lack the ability to make a strong assertion and defend their position. They cannot form a persuasive argument in either word or speech.

> *"We fail lamentably on the whole in teaching them how to think; they learn everything, except the art of learning...*

> *"...The whole of the trivium was, in fact, intended to teach the pupil the proper use of the tools of learning, before he began to apply them to "subjects" at all. First, he learned a language; not just how to order a meal in a foreign language, but the structure of language — a language, and hence of language itself — what it was, how it was put together, and how it worked.*

> *"Secondly, he learned how to make accurate statements; how to construct an argument and how to detect fallacies in argument (his own arguments and other people's). Dialectic, that is to say, embraced logic and disputation.*

> *"Thirdly, he learned to express himself in language; how to say what he had to say elegantly and persuasively. At the end of his course, he was required to compose a thesis upon some theme set by his masters or chosen by himself, and afterwards to defend his thesis against the criticism of the faculty. By this time he would have learned — or woe betide him — not merely to write an essay on paper, but to speak audibly and intelligibly from a platform, and to use his wits quickly when heckled. There would be questions, cogent and*

shrewd, from those who had already run the gauntlet of debate...

"Medieval education concentrated on first forging and learning to handle the tools of learning, using whatever subject came handy as a piece of material on which to doodle until the use of the tool became second nature."

Dorothy L. Savers, *The Lost Tools of Learning*

It is very important to note that the third stage of the trivium relies heavily upon the proper formation of the two earlier stages:

"Rhetoric is dependent upon the first two stages of the trivium, the grammar stage laid a foundation of knowledge; without knowledge, the rhetorician has nothing of substance to say. The Logic stage taught the students to think through the validity of arguments, to weigh the value of evidence. In the Rhetoric stage, the student uses knowledge and the skill of logical argument to write and speak about all the subjects in the curriculum."

Jessie Wise & Susan Wise Bauer,
A Well Trained Mind

The Quadrivium

"A human being should be able to change a diaper, plan an invasion, butcher a hog, conn a ship, design a building, write a sonnet, balance accounts, build a wall, set a bone, comfort the

> *dying, take orders, give orders, cooperate, act alone, solve equations, analyze a new problem, pitch manure, program a computer, cook a tasty meal, fight efficiently, die gallantly. Specialization is for insects."*
>
> Robert A Heinlein, *Time Enough For Love*

Historically, the quadrivium represented the four-fold teaching of Music, Numbers (of themselves), Geometry (numbers occupying space), and Astronomy. A year of study was dedicated to each subject. Due to the vast expansion of the arts and sciences, the idea of the quadrivium has become somewhat obsolete. However, this stage represents the beginning of the age of specialization and occupations with a particular subject above all others.

> *"The medieval quadrivium was the fore-runner of our university, and is the reason today that earning an undergraduate degree still requires a four-year course of study."*
>
> *Encyclopedia Brittanica*
> on the History of Education

The Subjects of Grammar, Dialectic & Rhetoric

> *"What is Classical Education? It is language-intensive-not-image-focused. It demands that students use and understand words, not video images. It is history-intensive, providing students with a comprehensive view of human endeavor from the beginning until now. It trains the mind to analyze and draw conclusions. It demands self-discipline. It produces literate, curious, intelligent*

students who have a wide range of interests and the ability to follow up on them."

Jessie Wise & Susan Wise Bauer,
A Well Trained Mind

Grammar: Mastery of the elements of a language

"Over fifty percent of English vocabulary comes from Latin. Over eighty percent of the vocabulary of the Romance languages (Portuguese, Spanish, French, Italian, Romanian) comes from Latin because the Romance languages are Roman languages. They are all simply corrupted forms of Latin. So, if you learn Latin it is a wonderful platform from which to decide which Romance language you are going to study. You can go in any number of directions. And if you never pursue any foreign language at all it is a tremendous help with your English vocabulary."

Doug Wilson, during an interview
by Michael Holloway, 1994

Logic: Mastery of statements, definitions, arguments and fallacies

"Logic is the art of arguing correctly: `If A, then B'; the method is not invalidated by the hypothetical character of A. Indeed, the practical utility of Formal Logic today lies not so much in the establishment of positive conclusions as in the prompt detection and exposure of invalid inference."

Dorothy L. Sayers, *The Lost Tools of Learning*

Rhetoric: Mastery of creative and persuasive speech

"Aristotle, who lived at roughly the same time as Alexander the Great, compiled the system of formal Logic in use today and wrote a treatise on Rhetoric used in universities for millenia."

"The occupation of rhetorician, or public-speaker, was a lofty one in Roman society, with Cicero being the most renown. Quintilian, who was influenced by Cicero, was a famous teacher of rhetoric in Rome and wrote Institutio Oratoria, a work detailing the instruction of children and the training of orators; it was likewise used for centuries."

Encyclopedia Brittanica
on the History of Education

A Sense of "Mastery"

Education is not mastered at the end of a semester, year, or program. It is mastered when the tools of learning are comfortable and well-worn.

"The primary goal of Classical Education... is to equip educated men and women able to approach previously unknown subject matter, problems, or life situations; and using the tools of learning which have been practiced and refined and internalized in school; to grasp the subject or problem, analyze it according to the standard of truth, and understand and do something about it. Classical Education therefore trains children for success in

any field, whether it be marriage and family life, work dealing with society and individuals, business, or arts and the humanities."

Otto Willmann, *The Seven Liberal Arts*

"For the tools of learning are the same, in any and every subject; and the person who knows how to use them will, at any age, get the mastery of a new subject in half the time and with a quarter of the effort expended by the person who has not the tools at his command. To learn six subjects without remembering how they were learnt does nothing to ease the approach to a seventh; to have learnt and remembered the art of learning makes the approach to every subject an open door.

"We have lost the tools of learning — the axe and the wedge, the hammer and the saw, the chisel and the plane — that were so adaptable to all tasks. Instead of them, we have merely a set of complicated jigs, each of which will do but one task and no more, and in using which eye and hand receive no training, so that no man ever sees the work as a whole or "looks to the end of the work." What use is it to pile task on task and prolong the days of labor, if at the close the chief object is left unattained?

Dorothy L. Savers, *The Lost Tools of Learning*

"The perpetual student syndrome is the exact opposite of the classical ideal. Continual reliance on educational institutions does not show a dedication to learning, but the fact that one has never

really acquired the skills of learning, but just an amalgamation of subjects. It is shocking how often you see people traipsing off to the local community college to learn some subject they could very easily acquire by spending a couple of evenings with the right books. If a teacher has not taught his students to learn for themselves, he can only be seen as a failure. Sadly, we tend to equate the level of someone's education with the amount of time they have spent in the academic institutions, rather than by how quickly they come to be free of the need for those institutions."

Fritz Hinrichs, *Classical Worldview*

Resources for More Information

A Catholic Homeschool Treasury, by Rachel Mackson and Maureen Willmann

Another Sort of Learning, by James V. Schall

Classical Education, by Gene Edward Veith, Jr. and Andrew Kern

Classical Education & The Home School, by Douglas Wilson, Wesley Callihan, & Douglas Jones

Designing Your Own Classical Curriculum, by Laura M. Berquist

Marva Collins' Way, by Marva Collins and Civia Tamarkin

Norms and Nobility: A Treatise on Education, David Hicks

Paideia of God, by Douglas Wilson

Recovering the Lost Tools of Learning, by Douglas Wilson

Repairing the Ruins, edited by Douglas Wilson

The Abolition of Man, by C.S. Lewis

The Devil Knows Latin, by E. Christian Kopff
The Lost Tools of Learning, by Dorothy Sayers
The Seven Laws of Teaching, by John Milton Gregory
The Well Trained Mind, by Jessie Wise and Susan Wise
Bauer

SIMILARITIES AND DIFFERENCES

There is some debate between "Charlotte Mason Purists" and "Classical Education Purists" that these methods are by nature diametrically opposed. Some people feel that Charlotte Mason was an "unschooler". They argue that Charlotte, fed up with the very standards imposed by traditional classical education, developed her philosophy as a "near-opposite" view of the Classical method.

However, the subjects and manner of teaching that Charlotte employed hint that she may have used the trivium. If we keep in mind that Classical Education was the standard at that time, it is easy to suppose that she might have recorded only the aspects with which she disagreed in her books, while employing other "Classical" methods in her philosophy without either acknowledgement or criticism.

Certainly Charlotte advocated against "twaddle" and "dull facts", but she also taught her students the rigorous grammar of Latin, French, and German at an early age. Clearly Charlotte taught subjects that required tremendous discipline and repetition, and it is not too much to suppose that she took advantage of the "Poll-parrot stage" to cover grammar lessons.

In any case, there are a number of similarities between these two philosophies, not the least of which is that they both believed in a "Liberal Arts" education. Whether or not Charlotte Mason would object to modern homeschoolers draping the "comfortable home-made quilt" style of her approach over the "well-fashioned chair" approach of a Classical Education we can only speculate. For those who like to pick and choose at ideas, there is a great deal to be gleaned from both methods.

Great Books

Charlotte Mason and the Classical Education method both recommend using "great books." Great books are, in fact, the backbone of both philosophies.

> *"Take all the words available in the human vocabulary and read them from the dictionary and you have only a list of words. But with the creativity and imagination God has given human beings, let these words flow together in the right order and they give wings to the spirit. Every child ought to know the pleasure of words so well chosen that they awaken sensibility, great emotion, and understanding of truth. This is the magic of words— touch of the supernatural, communication, which ministers to the spirit, a gift of God."*
>
> Gladys Hunt, *Honey for a Child's Heart*

> *"As believing Christians, our desire should be to do everything we do to the glory of God. This means we should not write, and we should not read Christian books which are a bunch of nothing. A Christian literature program is not one in which the students read `Christian books.' A Christian literature program is one in which the students are taught to read great literature, and are to think while they read, as Christians."*
>
> Doug Wilson

"When you re-read a classic, you do not see more in the book than you did before, you see more in you than was there before."

Clifton Fadiman

"To begin with, I kept books everywhere in the house; we had books for presents... and I was known at the local public library as `the lady with the laundry basket' because I took my children in every week and filled a laundry basket with their books."

Jessie Wise & Susan Wise Bauer,
A Well Trained Mind

Great Minds

Mortimer J. Alder calls the "great conversation" the "ongoing conversation of great minds down through the ages. You get in touch with these `minds' by reading their books."

"Books are the legacies that a great genius leaves to mankind, which are delivered down from generation to generation, as presents to the posterity of those who are yet unborn."

Addison, *The Spectator*

"Poets and writers shape the minds of generations — whether for good or ill. But here we prove ourselves to be virtually without letters. We, the people of the Word, ought to be masters of words; Christians ought to be preeminent in word-

smithing. We are not. In this hour of crisis, we produce and sell mountains of smarmy goo and oceans of treacle. We wouldn't know a great book if it ran naked through the CBA convention."

Doug Wilson

"Each of us, when we read a book, looks over someone's shoulder, trying to figure out the other, hoping to see what another sees, grubbing for a clue as to what is going on in the world, delighting in the experience of living through someone else's life, if just for a few hours."

William H. Willimon

"Why read? Leo Strauss, in a memorable remark, noted that we are lucky if more than one or two great minds are alive in the generations during which we are ourselves alive. This meant, in Strauss' view, that we would have to encounter the greatest minds mostly in books. Strauss, himself one of the great teachers of our century, is worth citing here: Teachers themselves are pupils and must be pupils. But there cannot be an infinite regress. Ultimately there must be teachers who are not in turn pupils. Those teachers who are not in turn pupils are the great minds or, in order to avoid any ambiguity in a matter of such importance, the greatest minds. Such men are extremely rare. We are not likely to meet any of them in any classroom. We are not likely to meet any of them anywhere. It is a piece of good luck if there is a single one alive in one's time. for all practical purposes, pupils, of whatever degree of

proficiency, have access to the teachers who are not in turn pupils, to the greatest minds, only through the great books. Liberal education will then consist in studying with proper care the great books which the greatest minds have left behind."

"This consideration about the importance of reading the great books to confront the greatest minds needs, however, to be recalled in the context of the fact that at least two of the most important human beings that ever lived, Socrates and Christ, did not write any book at all. They did, nevertheless, have scribes or students who listened carefully to what they said. The records of these sayings and reflections constitute some of the most precious readings that we possess, on which much of our particular civilization, on which civilization itself, rests. Not to know or possess these books is not to have begun any serious intellectual endeavor."

James V. Schall, *Another Sort of Learning*

A Goal of Self-Education (Mastery)

The goal of an education should not be, as some think, to receive a certificate, diploma, or even a degree. Both the Classical and Charlotte Mason methods teach that students must eventually take responsibility for their own education, and that education is a life-long process.

"You'll find children are on the road to `self-education.'" wrote Catherine Levison, regarding Charlotte Mason's way of teaching. Dorothy Sayers concurred, saying of the Classical approach that it would "teach men how to learn for themselves; and whatever instruction fails to do this is effort spent in vain."

Increasing Popularity Among Homeschoolers

Both the Charlotte Mason method and Classical Education are enjoying renewed interest and attention. Much of this attention has come from homeschooling parents who are seeking an academically strong, yet child-sensitive method of educating their children.

Parents, reading on the subject of education, will eventually come across a "Liberal Arts" method. They will be given pause to consider that education is not simply the means to a vocational end, but the liberation of the mind through the tools of learning.

The Charlotte Mason and Classical methods of education blend together so well, and are so adaptable to homeschoolers, that it seems the combination of these methods is inevitable.

THE CHARLOTTE MASON-CLASSICAL EDUCATION APPROACH

What Does a Typical Day Look Like?

Homeschooling methods are, by definition, as unique as the homes they come from. As I share my choice of subjects and my schedule, please be aware that I include it only for information's sake. It is not intended to be copied or taken as "the" method. It is simply a schedule that worked for me.

I used this particular schedule when I operated my "school" in Washington State. (I obtained legal permission to homeschool other people's children due to special circumstances.) At one time, I had one child from public school. Five children came from one family who had been homeschooled all their lives, but the mom was expecting another child and was feeling overwhelmed and needed help. I also had one very high-functioning autistic 3rd grade child who did very well using this approach.

I followed Charlotte Mason's recommendation of doing school in the morning. This left free time in the afternoon for playing outside or pursuing other activities. Children learn by doing, so there must be "free" time allotted for this purpose. This is also a good time for nature walks.

The children worked from eight in the morning through to lunchtime, with no breaks. That may sound tedious, but the lessons were short and varied, and the children never had time to be bored or to dawdle. In fact, we had fun! The trick is to vary the subjects and keep them short.

Charlotte Mason believed that a child should start with math, so that is how we spent our first 20 minutes. Then we moved to history. The children read for about 13 minutes (Charlotte said that this is a good period of time), and then I had one child reiterate what he had read. The children never knew which one would be chosen for this, so they would all pay attention in case they were the one picked.

We spent the next 15 or so minutes doing English, followed by another 15 minutes of historical fiction. Again, I would choose one of the children to "re-tell" what was read. Then, we would do either poetry or Latin, depending on what day it was (15 minutes). Science was next. We spent about 20 minutes either reading or doing an experiment. This was followed by Spanish (10 minutes), spelling (5 minutes), music (15 minutes), and art (15 minutes). Finally, we would have what I called a "class make-up" time, because each student also took piano on a rotating basis, and each had missed a different subject that now needed to be made up. Our school day usually lasted about three hours and forty-five minutes. This included extra time used here and there — in between subjects, or when one subject took longer than expected.

I used the Suzuki method for piano, taught by a qualified instructor once per week, with lesson practice every day. The Suziki teaching method seemed to be the best suited to the Charlotte Mason philosophy and the way that the children learned. It seemed that playing the piano really did make a difference in how well children performed in other subjects, especially in math. If I'd had children in the dialectic or rhetoric stages, I would have taught logic (in eighth grade) and rhetoric in high school.

I have followed many of Charlotte's methods, but I also incorporate the Classical Education approach. I do this by employing the strategic use of the three stages of learning – concentrating on memorizing at an early age, and expecting more thoughtful work from an older child, for example. I also teach with an underlying expectation of great things. In the vein of Classical Education, I expect that a child can not only "handle" Beethoven, but also love it. (Charlotte Mason would have agreed.)

Setting up a precise schedule is not as important as determining the direction that your teaching will take. I believe that one can teach in the Charlotte Mason or Classical Education modes at any time of day, and with a huge variety of subjects. The key is to make the goal of education "self-education", and to instill a love of learning. This is really the emphasis of both methods.

What Do I Do If I've Missed the Grammar Stage?

Education progressives claim that knowledge is changing so rapidly that what children learn today will be outdated tomorrow; that schools therefore can at best only teach them "accessing skills," such as how to surf the Internet. But such a rationale does a grave disservice to children, because there is a body of bedrock knowledge — pivotal events in world history, the development of constitutional government, principles of writing and mathematics. And there are masterworks of art, music, and literature — with which they should be familiar in order to be fulfilled individuals.

Public Charter Schools and the
Core Knowledge Movement,
The Lexington Institute, Arlington, Virginia

For those who have homeschooled their children for a few years, but are evolving toward Classical Education or the combined approach, the question of "missing" the grammar stage is an important one. The Classical method builds on a strong foundation of factual knowledge. In fact, much of the teaching geared toward the primary grades has more to do with memorization than with self-expression. So, switching to the Classical method after grades 3 or 4 could be challenging, but only because it isn't learned as easily.

The best approach for parents in this position is to first determine any area or subject in which their children may be lacking. For example, a typical Classical foundation for a child completing grade three might include:

- Memorization of the Presidents (Prime Ministers, in Canada) and pieces of political significance (Declaration of Independence, for example)
- Memorization of the States (or Provinces) and Capitals, the continents, and major geographical landforms (rivers, deserts, oceans)
- Extensive grammar and language study

- Basic math facts (times tables, fractions, etc.)
- Basic science facts (water cycle, food chain, names of planets, types of local trees, insects, and birds, etc.)

In addition, Classically educated children may have been exposed to famous artists, sculptors, poets, and writers. They may have had musical or foreign language training. Some students may be able to recite large works of poetry, or name the entire scientific table of the elements.

For those trying to change horses in the middle of the river, this can all be quite intimidating. However, we must again remind ourselves what the goal and purpose of the switching is — it is to train up a child in the ways of learning, so that he can eventually become self-taught, and it is to feed the fire of knowledge, so that the joy of learning is never quenched.

With this in mind, it is easy to see that the table of the elements can always be memorized later, and even basic math facts can still be learned if by chance they have been missed (although it may be more difficult and time consuming).

The grammar stage is simply an *opportunity* to pour knowledge into a child, because they are so open for the pouring at that age. And when this well of knowledge is present, it can be drawn upon easily in every circumstance of need. But it is not absolutely necessary. Both the Charlotte Mason and Classical Education approaches can be used with children of any age. As far as Classical Education goes, simply recognize the age and stage of your child, and teach to that stage as best you can. For the Charlotte Mason approach, follow her guidelines of reading classic literature, appreciating nature and great art, and instilling a love of life and learning. The rest will follow.

Part II
Book Lists and Resources by Subject

HISTORY

World History

For the most part, individual books on each subject will not be listed here, as there are already so many good book-lists available. A listing of "books with book lists" is presented later in this book. Homeschool groups, public libraries, and many websites can be great sources for book lists, too.

When studying history, look first for biographies and historical fiction. Use these in conjunction with a book that provides an overview of world history. If using a textbook, try to find one written by a single author. Some good "over-all" world history books include:

> *A History of the English Speaking Peoples,* by Winston S. Churchill. This is a series of volumes.
> *Modern Times, The World from the Twenties to the Nineties*, by Paul Johnson is a distinguished book of more recent history.
> *A Child's History of the World* by V.M. Hillyer, is a book, which younger children will enjoy.
> *The Kingfisher Illustrated History of the World* is also very good, but is not written by one author.

It is in the use of biographies and historical fiction that the facts will come alive, so choose some areas of specific interest, and locate some of these books to compliment your study.

Landmark books produced some wonderful historical fiction and biographies designed for children from fourth grade through junior high. There were originally over two hundred titles, but there are only about a dozen titles still in print. However, they are worth looking for in used-book stores and libraries. A list of titles is included on the following page.

Please Note: Many of the books listed in this section are no longer in print, but have been included because they are excellent resources, and can still be found in used bookstores. The author, Jenny Sockey, operates a used-book service via her website. She specializes in books pertaining to the Charlotte Mason and Classical Education methods. If you would like more information about any of the books listed in this section, or would like help finding an out-of-print book, visit Jenny's website: (**Charlotte's Classical USED BOOKshelf**) http://www.JennySockey.com or Contact Jenny at cmandce@JennySockey.com.

Also, the **Homeschool Potpourri** bookstore (now owned by the author's daughter, Colleen Aukland, and her husband, Todd Aukland) may have some of these titles in stock. Contact them at (425) 820-4626, or visit their website at www.homeschoolpotpourri.com..

World History—"Landmarks" Series

Note: Most of the original hardcovers have the "W" number somewhere on the book, "W" representing "world". The numbers have been included to make the books easier for collectors to find.

W1	*The First Men in the World,* by Anne Terry White
W2	*Alexander the Great,* by John Gunther
W3	*Adventures & Discoveries of Marco Polo,* by Richard J. Walsh
W4	*Joan of Arc,* by Nancy Wilson Ross
W5	*King Arthur and His Knights,* by Mabel Louise Robinson
W6	*Mary, Queen of Scotts,* by Emily Hahn
W7	*Napoleon and the Battle of Waterloo,* by Frances Winwar
W8	*Royal Canadian Mounted Police,* by Richard

L. Neuberger

W9 *The Man Who Changed China: The Story of Sunyat-Sen,* by Pearl S. Buck

W10 *The Battle of Britain*, by Quentin Reynolds

W11 *The Crusades*, by Anthony West

W12 *Genghis Kahn and the Mongol Horde*, by Harold Lamb

W13 *Queen Elizabeth and the Spanish Armada*, by Fances Winwar

W14 *Simon Bolivar, The Great Liberator*, by Arnold Whitridge

W15 *The Slave Who Freed Haiti: The Story of Tuussaint Louverture*, by Katherine Scherman

W16 *The Story of Scotland Yard*, by Laurence Thompson

W17 *The Life of Saint Patrick*, by Quentin Reynolds

W18 *The Exploits of Xenophon*, by Geoffrey Household

W19 *Captain Cook Explores the South Seas*, by Armstrong Sperry

W20 *Marie Antoinette*, by Bernadine kielty

W21 *Will Shakespeare and the Globe Theater*, by Anne Terry White

W22 *The French Foreign Legion*, by Wyatt Blassingame

W23 *Martin Luther*, by Harry Emerson Fosdick

W24 *The Hudson's Bay Company*, by Richard Morenus

W25 *Balboa: Swordsman and Conquistador*, by Felix Riesenberg

W26 *The Magna Charta*, by James Daugherty

W27 *Leonardo Da Vinci*, by Emily Hahn

W28 *General Brock and Niagara Falls*, by Samuel Hopkins Adams

W29 *Catherine the Great*, by Katherine Scherman

W30 *The Fall of Constantinople*, by Bernadine Kielty

W31 *Ferdinand Magellan: Master Mariner*, by Seymour Gates Pond

W32 *Garibaldi: Father of Modern Italy*, by Marcia Davenport

W33 *The Story of Albert Schweitzer*, by Anita Daniel

W34 *The Marquis de Lafayette: Bright Sword for Freedom*, by Hodding Carter

W35 *Famous Pirates of the New World*, by A.B.C. Whipple

W36 *Exploring the Himalayas*, by William O. Douglas

W37 *Queen Victoria*, by Noel Streatfeild

W38 *The Flight and Adventures of Charles II*, by Charles Norman

W39 *Chief of the Cossacks*, by Harold Lamb

W40 *Adventures of Ulysses*, by Gerald Gottlief

W41 *William the Conqueror*, by Thomas B. Costain

W42 *Jesus of Nazareth*, by Harry Emerson Fosdick

W43 *Julius Caesar*, by John Gunther

W44 *The Story of Australia*, by A. Grove Day

W45 *Captain Cortes Conquers Mexico*, by William Johnson

W46 *Florence Nightingale*, by Ruth Fox Hume

W47 *The Rise and Fall of Adolf Hitler*, by William L. Shirer

W48 *The Story of Atomic Energy*, by Laura Fermi

W49 *Great Men of Science*, by Ruth Fox Hume

W50 *Cleopatra of Egypt*, by Leonora Hornblow

W51 *The Sinking of the Bismarck*, by William L. Shirer

W52 *Lawrence of Arabia*, by Alistair MacLean

W53 *The Life of Saint Paul*, by Harry Emerson Fosdick

W54   *The Voyages of Henry Hudson*, by Eugene Rachlis

W55   *Hero of Trafalgar: Story of Lord Nelson*, by A.B.C. Whipple

W56   *Winston Churchill*, by Quentin Reynolds

W57   *The War in Korea: 1950-1953*, by Robert Leckie

W58   *Walter Raleigh: Man of Two Worlds*, by Henrietta Buckmaster

W59   *The Pharoahs of Ancient Egypt*, by Elizabeth Payne

W60   *Flying Aces of World War I*, by Gene Gurney

W61   *Commandos of World War II*, by Hodding Carter

W62   *Ben Gurion and the Birth of Israel*, by Joan Comay

W63   *The United Nations in War and Peace*, by T.R. Fehrenbach

World History—"We Were There" Series

Another good series for world history is the *We Were There* series. Here are some of the titles:

We Were There at Pearl Harbor
We Were There at the Battle for Bataan
We Were There at the Battle of Gettysburg
We Were There at the Battle of Lexington and Concord
We Were There at the Battle of the Alamo
We Were There at the Battle of the Bulge
We Were There at the Driving of the Golden Spike
We Were There at the First Airplane Flight
We Were There at the Normandy Invasion
We Were There at the Oklahoma Land Run
We Were There at the Opening of the Atomic Era
We Were There at the Opening of the Erie Canal

We Were There in the Klondike Gold Rush
We Were There on the Chisolm Trail
We Were There on the Nautilus
We Were There on the Oregon Trail
We Were There on the Santa Fe Trail
We Were There with Byrd at the South Pole
We Were There with Ethan Allen and the Green
     Mountain Boys
We Were There with Lewis and Clark
We Were There with Lincoln in the White House
We Were There with Caesar's Legions
We Were There with Richard the Lionhearted in the
     Crusades
We Were There with the California 49'ers
We Were There with the California Rancheros
We Were There with the Mayflower Pilgrims
We Were There with the Pony Express
We Were There at the Battle of Britain
We Were There at the Boston Tea Party
We Were There when Grant Met Lee at Appomattox
We Were There when Washington Won at Yorktown
We Were There with Charles Darwin on H.M.S. Beagle
We Were There with Cortes and Montezuma
We Were There with Florence Nightingale in the Crimea
We Were There with Jean Lafitte at New Orleans
We Were There with the Lafayette Escadrille

World History—"Great Lives Observed" Series

Each volume in this series views the character and achievement of a great world figure in three perspectives—through his own words, through the opinions of his contemporaries, and through retrospective judgments - thus combining the intimacy of autobiography, the immediacy of eyewitness observation, and the objectivity of modern scholarship.

The American Story, by Morton and Penn Borden
Bismark, by Frederic B. M. Hollyday
John C Calhoun, by Margaret L. Coit
Catherine The Great, by L. Jay Oliva
Churchill, by Martin Gilbert
Cromwell, by Maurice Ashley
Debs, by Ronald Radosh
Frederick Douglass, by Benjamin Quarles
Elizabeth I, by Joseph M. Levine
Henry Ford, by John B. Rae
Frederick the Great, by Louis L. Snyder
Garibaldi, by Denis Mack Smith
William Lloyd Garrison, by George M. Fredrickson
Gompers, by Gerald Emanuel Stearn
Hamilton, by Milton Cantor
Hitler, by George H Stein
Jefferson, by Adrienne Koch
Jesus, by Hugh Anderson
La Follette, by Robert S Maxwell
Lenin, by Saul N Silverman
Lloyd George, by Martin Gilbert
Huey Long, by High Davis Graham
MacArthur, by Lawrence S. Wittner
Joseph R. McCarthy, by Allen J. Matusow
Mao, by Jerome Ch'en
John Marshall, by Stanley I. Kutler
Napoleon, by Maurice Hutt
Peter The Great, by L. Jay Oliva
Robespierre, by George Rude
Franklin Delano Roosevelt, by Gerald D. Nash
Theodore Roosevelt, by Dewey W. Grantham
Stalin, by T. H. Rigby
Nat Turner, by Eric Foner
Denmark Vesey: The Slave Conspiracy of 1822, by
        Robert S Starobin

Booker T. Washington, by Emma Lou Thornbrough
George Washington, by Morton Borden

World History—Other Resources

Follow the Landmark series with volumes by G.A. Henty. These volumes are more challenging and are better suited to older children. G. A. Henty was a nineteenth century minister whose father and grandfather were historians by trade. The other historians of his time thought that he was extremely accurate. Henty's secretary got tired of hearing him tell these great stories to his children and grandchildren, and told him to write them down. He did, and they are wonderful. They are finally being republished by Preston Speed Publications.

G.A. Henty lovers may be interested in purchasing a copy of the *Henty Companion,* by Hugh Pruen. It has resumes of all of Henty's books with valuable cross-references. (Check with *Homeschool Potpourri* or another bookstore for a copy.)

History can be made more interesting by adding to it the study of geography. An excellent book is, "Around the World in 180 Days" by Sherrie Payne. This book is published by Apologia Educational Ministries Inc. (They also have a good science curriculum, which will be mentioned later.) This is a multi-grade guide for the study of world history and cultures. It uses the notebook approach to studying the geography, history, culture and current events of all seven continents.

Under each continent, Ms. Payne has listed:
* Resource List
* Geography
* History
* Religion
* Culture
* Current Events.

This book adapts well to homeschooling, as children of various ages can learn at once. The book can be modified slightly to reflect a more Classical approach: change the order of the study of the continents to Asia, Africa, Europe, South America, North America, Australia and Antarctica, and spend up to a year on each one, following the events of history as you go. Add biographies and historical fiction for specific areas of interest and depth.

American History

For an overview of American history, choose books written by a single author. Joy Hakim did not like the textbooks used by her children's teachers, so she developed her own from diaries and such. Her series, *A History of the United States* (Oxford University Press) is very good, but naturally the bias of the author comes across in her writing. (Ms. Hakim appears to have a dislike of President Reagan).

Another interesting book is a *Quest of a Hemisphere* by Donzella Cross Boyle (Western Islands Publishing, 1970). This book is no longer being published, but is worth hunting for in a used-book store or library.

A History of the American People, by Paul Johnson (currently published by HarperCollins) is also an excellent book.

Of course, the Landmark series for American history is excellent.

American History—"Landmark" Series

Again, many of these are out of print, but are worth looking for in used bookstores and libraries. Hard covers may or may not have the number on them.

1)   *The Voyages of Christopher Columbus*, by Armstron Sperry

2) *The Landing of the Pilgrims*, by James Daugherty
3) *Pocahontas & Captain John Smith*, by Marie Lawson
4) *Paul Revere & The Minute Men*, by Dorothy Canfield Fisher
5) *Our Independence and the Constitution*, by Dorothy Canfield Fisher
6) *The California Gold Rush*, by May McNeer
7) *The Pony Express*, by Samuel Hopkins Adams
8) *Lee and Grant at Appomattox*, by Mackinlay Kantor
9) *The Building of the first Transcontinental Railroad*, by Adele Gutman Nathan
10) *The Wright Brothers*, by Quentin Reynolds
11) *Prehistoric America*, by Anne Terry White
12) *The Vikings*, by Elizabeth Janeway
13) *The Santa Fe Trail*, by Samuel Hopkins Adams
14) *The Story of the U.S. Marines*, by George Hunt
15) *The Lewis and Clark Expedition*, by Richard L. Neuberger
16) *The Monitor and the Merrimac*, by Fletcher Pratt
17) *The Explorations of Pere Marquette*, by Jim Kjelgaard
18) *The Panama Canal*, by Bob Considine
19) *The Pirate LaFitte and the Battle of the New Orleans*, by Robert Tallant
20) *Custer's Last Stand*, by Quentin Reynolds
21) *Daniel Boone*, by John Mason Brown
22) *Clipper Ship Days*, by John Jennings
23) *Gettysburg*, by MacKinlay Kantor
24) *The Louisiana Purchase*, by Robert Tallant
25) *Wild Bill Hickok Tames the West*, by Stewart H. Holbrook
26) *Betsy Ross and the Flag*, by Jane Mayer
27) *The Conquest of the North and South Poles*, by Russell Owen

28) *Ben Franklin of Old Philadelphia*, by Margaret Cousins
29) *Trappers and Traders of the Far West*, by James Daugherty
30) *Mr. Bell Invents the Telephone*, by Katherine B. Shippen
31) *The Barbary Pirates*, by C.S. Forester
32) *Sam Houston, The Tallest Texan*, by William Johnson
33) *The Winter at Valley Forge*, by Van Wyck Nason
34) *The Erie Canal*, by Samuel Hopkins Adams
35) *Thirty Seconds over Tokyo*, by Ted lawson & Bob Considine
36) *Thomas Jefferson, Father of Democracy*, by Vincent Sheean
37) *The Coming of the Mormons*, by Jim Kjelgaard
38) *George Washington Carver, The Story of a Great American*, by Anne Terry White
39) *John Paul Jones, Fighting Sailor*, by Armstrong Sperry
40) *The First Overland Mail*, by Robert Pinkerton
41) *Teddy Roosevelt and the Rough Riders*, by Henry Castor
42) *To California by Covered Wagon*, by George R. Stewart
43) *Peter Stuyvesant of Old New York*, by Anna Erskine & Russell Crouse
44) *Lincoln and Douglas: The Years of Decision*, by Regina Z. Kelly
45) *Robert Fulton and the Steamboat*, by Ralph Nading Hill
46) *The F.B.I.*, by Quentin Reynolds
47) *Dolly Madison*, by Jane Mayer
48) *John James Audubon*, by Margaret & John Kieran
49) *Hawaii, Gem of the Pacific*, by Oscar Lewis

50) *War Chief of the Seminoles*, by May McNeer
51) *Old Ironsides, The Fighting Constitution*, by Harry Hansen
52) *The Mississippi Bubble*, by Thomas B. Costain
53) *Kit Carson and the Wild Frontier*, by Ralph Moody
54) *Robert E. Lee and the Road of Honor*, by Hodding Carter
55) *Guadalcanal Diary*, by Richard Tregaskis
56) *Commodore Perry and the Opening of Japan*, by Ferdinand Kuhn
57) *Davy Crockett*, by Stewart H. Holbrook
58) *Clara Barton, Founder of the American Red Cross*, by Helen Boylston
59) *The Story of San Francisco*, by Charlotte Jackson
60) *Up the Trail from Texas*, by Frank Dobie
61) *Abe Lincoln: Log Cabin to White House*, by Sterlig North
62) *The Story of D_Day: June 6, 1944*, by Bruce Bliven, Jr.
63) *Roger's Rangers and the French and Indian War*, by Bradford Smith
64) *The World's Greatest Showman: The Life of P.T. Barnum*, by Joe Bryan
65) *Sequoyah: Leader of the Cherokees*, by Alice Marriott
66) *Ethen Allen and the Green Mountain Boys*, by Slater Brown
67) *Wyatt Earp: U.S. Marshall*, by Stewart H. Holbrook
68) *The Early Days of Automobiles*, by Elizabeth Janeway
69) *The Witchcraft of Salem Village*, by Shirley Jackson
70) *The West Point Story*, by Col. Red and Nardi Reeder Campion

71) *George Washington: Frontier Colonel*, by Walter Havighurst
72) *The Texas Rangers*, by Will Henry
73) *Buffalo Bill's Great Wild West Show*, by Walter Havighurst
74) *Evangeline and the Acadians*, by Robert Tallant
75) *The Story of the Secret Service*, by Ferdinand Kuhn
76) *Tippecanoe and Tyler, Too!* By Stanley Young
77) *America's First World War: General Pershing and the Yanks*, by Henry Castor
78) *The Doctors Who Conquered Yellow Fever*, by Ralph Nading Hill
79) *Remember the Alamo!* by Robert Penn Warren
80) *Andrew Carnegie and the Age of Steel*, by Katherine B. Shippen
81) *Geronimo: Wolf of the Warpath*, by Ralph Moody
82) *The Story of the Paratroops*, by George Weller
83) *The American Revolution*, by Bruce Bilven, Jr.
84) *The Story of the Naval Academy*, by Felix Riesenberg, Jr.
85) *Alexander Hamilton and Aaron Burr*, by Anna Erskine & Russell Crouse
86) *Stonewall Jackson*, by Jonathan Daniels
87) *The Battle for the Atlantic*, by Jay Williams
88) *The First Transatlantic Cable*, by Adele Gutman Nathan
89) *The Story of the U.S. Air Force*, by Robert Loomis
90) *The Swamp Fox of the Revolution*, by Stewart H. Holbrook
91) *Heroines of the Early West*, by Nancy Wilson Ross
92) *The Alaska Gold Rush*, by May McNeer
93) *The Golden Age of Railroads*, by Stewart H. Holbrook

94) *From Pearl Harbor to Okinawa*, by Bruce Bliven, Jr.
95) *The Copper Kings of Montana*, by Marian T. Place
96) *Great American Fighter Pilots of World War II*, by Robert D. Loomis
97) *The Story of the U.S. Coast Guard*, by Eugene Rachlis
98) *William Penn: Quaker Hero*, by Hildegarde Dolson
99) *John F. Kennedy and PT-109*, by Richard Tregaskis
100) *The Story of Oklahoma*, by Lon Tinkle
101) *Americans Into Orbit: The Story of Project Mercury*, by Gene Gurney
102) *The Story of Submarines*, by George Weller
103) *The Seabees of World War II*, by Edmund Castillo
104) *The U.S. Border Patrol*, by Clement Hellyer
105) *The Flying Tigers*, by John Toland
106) *The U.S. Frogmen of World War II*, by Edmund Castillo
107) *Women of Courage*, by Dorothy Nathan
108) *Dwight D. Eisenhower*, by Malcom Moos
109) *Disaster at Johnstown, The Great Flood*, by Hildegarde Dolson
110) *The Story of Thomas Alva Edison*, by Margaret Cousins
111) *Medal of Honor Heroes*, by Colonel Red Reeder
112) *From Casablanca to Berlin*, by Bruce Bliven
113) *Young Mark Twain and the Mississippi*, by Harnett T. Kane
114) *The Battle of the Bulge*, by John Toland
115) *The Story of the Thirteen Colonies*, by Clifford Lindsey
116) *Combat Nurses of World War II*, by Wyatt Blassingame

117) *Walk in Space, The Story of Project Gemini*, by Gene Gurney

118) *The Battle for Iwo Jima*, by Robert Leckie

119) *Midway, Battle for the Pacific*, by Captain Edmund L. Castillo, USN

120) *Medical Corps Heroes of World War II*, by Wyatt Blassingame

121) *Flat-Tops, The Story of Aircraft Carriers*, by Captain Edmund L. Castillo, USN

122) *The Mysterious Voyage of Captain Kidd*, by A.B.C. Whipple

American History—"Landmark Giants" Series

"Landmark Giant" books are bigger than the regular Landmark books. It is difficult to find a list of these titles. Here are the ones I have found:

1) *The F.B.I. Story*, by Don Whitehead

2) *The Continent We Live On*, by Ivan T. Sanderson

3) *The American Indian*, by William Brandon/Anne Terry White

4) *Story of Baseball*, by John McRosenberg

5) *Life in the Ancient World*, by Bart Winer

6) *Life in Colonial America*, by Elizabeth George Speare

7) *The Story of World War II*, by Robert Leckie

8) *Life in Lincoln's America*, by Helen Reeder Cross

9) *Story of Football*, by Robert Leckie

10) *Story of World War I*, by Robert Leckie

11) *Great American Athletes of the Twentieth Century*, by Zander Hollander

12) *Life in the Middle Ages*, by Jay Williams

13) *Washington DC—The Story of Our Nation's Capitol*, by Howard K. Smith

14) *American Heroes of the 20th Century*, by Harold & Doris Faber
15) *The Story of New England*, by Monroe Stearns
16) *The Landmark History of the American People, From Plymouth to Appomattox* (Volume One), by Daniel J. Boorstin with Ruth F. Boorstin (Now being published in paperback by Sonlight.)
17) *Great American Battles*, by Robert Leckie
18) *Life in the Renaissance*, by Gail Marzieh
19) *New York: The Story of the World's Most Exciting City*, by Bruce & Naomi Bliven
20) *Americans to the Moon, The Story of Project Apollo*, by Gene Gurney
21) *The Landmark History of the American People, From Appomattox to the Moon* (Volume Two), by Daniel J. Boorstin with Ruth F. Boorstin (Now being published in paperback by Sonlight.)
22) *American Sports Heroes of Today*, by Fred Katz
23) *Pro Football Heroes of Today*, by Berry Stainback
24) *Great Moments in American Sports*, by Jerry Brondfield
25) *Pro Hockey Heroes of Today*, by Bill Libby

American History—"Cornerstones of Freedom" Series

The *Cornerstones of Freedom* is another great series. Here is a chronological list courtesy of "Paula's archives" website: (www.PaulasArchives.com)

Before 1700

Christopher Columbus, by R. Conrad Stein
Jamestown Colony, by Gail Sakurai
Marquette and Jolliet, by R. Conrad Stein; Richard Wahl
Pilgrims, by R. Conrad Stein
Salem Witch Trials, by Zachary Kent

The Story of the Mayflower Compact, by Norman Richards

18th Century
African-Americans in the Thirteen Colonies, by Deborah Kent
Bill of Rights, by R. Conrad Stein
Boston Tea Party, by R. Conrad Stein
Constitution, by Marilyn Prolman
Declaration of Independence, by R. Conrad Stein or Norman Richards
Green Mountain Boys
Lexington and Concord, by R. Conrad Stein or Deborah Kent
Liberty Bell, by Gail Sakurai
Monticello, by Norman Richards
Mount Vernon, by Mary Collins
Paul Revere, by Gail Sakurai
Powers of the Congress, by R. Conrad Stein
Powers of the President, by R. Conrad Stein
Powers of the Supreme Court, by R. Conrad Stein
Valley Forge, by R. Conrad Stein
Surrender at Yorktown, by Zachary Kent
Thirteen Colonies, by Gail Sakurai
Williamsburg, by Zachary Kent

19th Century
African-Americans in the Old West, by Tom McGowen
Alamo, by Norman Richards
Arlington National Cemetery, by R. Conrad Stein
Asian Americans in the Old West, by Gail Sakurai
Assassination of Abraham Lincoln, by Brendan January
Barbary Pirates, by R. Conrad Stein (1805)
Battle of Antietam, by Zachary Kent
Battle of Bull Run, by Zachary Kent

Battle of Chancellorsville, by Zachary Kent
Battle of the Alamo, by Andrew Santella
Battle of the Little Bighorn, by R. Conrad Stein
Black Hawk War, by Jim Hargrove
Booker T. Washington, by Pat McKissack
Brooklyn Bridge, by Zachary Kent
Building the Capital City, by Marlene Targ Brill
California Gold Rush, by R. Conrad Stein
Changing White House, by Barbara Silberdick Feinberg
Chisholm Trail, by Andrew Santella
Clara Barton, by Zachary Kent
Dred Scott Decision, by Brendan January)
Election of Abraham Lincoln, by Zachary Kent
Ellis Island, by R. Conrad Stein
Emancipation Proclamation, by Brendan January
Ford's Theater and the Death of Lincoln, by Zachary
    Kent
Fort Sumter, by Brendan January
Geronimo, by Zachary Kent
Gettysburg Address, by Kenneth G. Richards
Harriet Beecher Stowe, by Maureen Ash
Haymarket Riot, by Charnan Simon
Homestead Act, by R. Conrad Stein
Industrial Revolution, by Mary Collins
Jane Addams and Hull House, by Deborah Kent
Jefferson Davis, by Zachery Kent
John Brown's Raid on Harpers Ferry, by January or
    Kent
Johnstown Flood, by R. Conrad Stein
Lewis and Clark, by R. Conrad Stein
Library of Congress, by Mary Collins
Lincoln Memorial, by Deborah Kent
Lincoln-Douglas Debates, by Brendan January
Little Bighorn, by R. Conrad Stein
Lone Star Republic, by R. Conrad Stein

Louisiana Purchase, by Gail Sakurai
Mapping the American West, by Judy Alter
Medicine in the Old West, by Lucile Davis
Mississippi Steamboats, by R. Conrad Stein
Natchez Trace, by Linda George
New England Whalers, by R. Conrad Stein
Old Ironsides, by Norman Richards
Oregon Trail, by R. Conrad Stein
Pony Express, by Peter Anderson
Pullman Strike, by R. Conrad Stein
Reconstruction, by Brendan January
Rough Riders, by Zachary Kent
Santa Fe Trail, by Judy Alter
Seward's Folly, by Susan Clinton
Sherman's March to the Sea, by Zachary Kent
Sinking of the Battleship Maine, by Zachary Kent
Spanish-American War, by Mary Collins
Star-Spangled Banner, by Deborah Kent
Nat Turners Rebellion, by Zachary Kent
Battle of Shiloh, by Zachary Kent
Burning of Washington, by R. Conrad Stein
Clipper Ships, by R. Conrad Stein
Erie Canal, by R. Conrad Stein
Surrender at Appomattox Court House, by Zachary Kent
Susan B. Anthony, by Susan Clinton
The Story of the Capitol, by Marilyn Prolman or by
     Andrew Santella
Trail of Tears, by R. Conrad Stein or Susan Clinton
Transcontinental Railroad, by Peter Anderson
Underground Railroad, by R. Conrad Stein
Unification of Germany, by Jim Hargrove
War of 1812, by Andrew Santella
Women Who Shaped the West, by Mary V. Fox
Wounded Knee, by R. Conrad Stein
Yellowstone National Park, by Deborah Kent

20th Century

Admiral Peary at the North Pole, by Zachary Kent
Alcatraz, by Linda George
Apollo 11, by R. Conrad Stein
Assassination of John F. Kennedy, by R. Conrad Stein
Assassination of Martin Luther King
Assassination of Robert F. Kennedy, by Andrew Santella
Battle for Iwo Jima, by Tom McGowen
Battle of Midway, by Tom McGowen
Battle of the Bulge, by R. Conrad Stein
Challenger Disaster, by Zachary Kent
Child Labor Laws, by R. Conrad Stein
Chuck Yeager Breaks the Sound Barrier, by R. Conrad Stein
Civil Rights Marches, by Linda George
Cold War, by Leila M. Foster
Cuban Missile Crisis, by Susan Maloney Clinton
D-Day, by R. Conrad Stein
Disability Rights Movement, by Deborah Kent
Empire State Building, by Patrick Clinton
Fall of the Soviet Union, by Miles Harvey
FBI, by Jim Hargrove
Flight at Kitty Hawk, by R. Conrad Stein
Franklin Delano Roosevelt Memorial, by Anne Phillips
Freedom Riders, by Deborah Kent
Golden Gate Bridge, by Sharlene P. Nelson
Great Depression, by R. Conrad Stein
Great Society, by Leila M. Foster
Henry Ford and the Automobile, by Zachary Kent
Hindenburg Disaster, by R. Conrad Stein
Hiroshima and Nagasaki, by Barbara Silberdick Feinberg
Impeachment, by Andrew Santella
Iran Hostage Crisis, by R. Conrad Stein
Jackie Robinson Breaks the Color Line, by Andrew Santella

Jonas Salk and the Discovery of Polio Vaccine, by Jim Hargrove

Kent State, by Arlene Erlbach

Korean War Veterans Memorial, by R. Conrad Stein

Live Aid, by Susan Clinton

Manhattan Project, by R. Conrad Stein

Mary McLeod Bethune, by Pat McKissack

Medal of Honor, by Roger Wachtel

Mississippi Flood of 1993, by Karin Luisa Badt

Montgomery Bus Boycott, by R. Conrad Stein

Mount Rushmore, by Andrew Santella

Names Project : AIDS Quilt, by Larry Dane Brimner

National Mall, by Brendan January

Panama Canal, by R. Conrad Stein or Winkelman

Peace Corps, by Zachary Kent

Persian Gulf War, by Leila Merrell Foster

Rachel Carson and the Environmental Movement, by Leila M. Foster

Roaring Twenties, by R. Conrad Stein

Saigon Airlift, by Zachary Kent

San Francisco Earthquake, by R. Conrad Stein

Spirit of St. Louis, by R. Conrad Stein

Statue of Liberty, by Natalie Miller

Lafayette Escadrille (WWI), by R. Conrad Stein

Nineteenth Amendment (Women's Suffrage), by R. Conrad Stein

Teapot Dome Scandal, by Jim Hargrove

Television, by Zachary Kent

The New York Stock Exchange, by Zachary Kent

The Story of Malcolm X, by Jack Slater

The Story of Television, by Zachary Kent

The Vietnam Women's Memorial, by Deborah Kent

Thomas Edison, by Nicholas Nirgiotis

Thurgood Marshall and the Supreme Court, by Deborah Kent

Times Square, by Wende Fazio
Titanic, by Deborah Kent
Triangle Factory Fire, by Zachary Kent
Tuskeegee Airmen, by Linda George
United Nations, by R. Conrad Stein
United States Holocaust Memorial Museum, by Philip Brooks
USS Arizona, by R. Conrad Stein
Vietnam Veterans Memorial, by Wright or Kent
Watergate, by Jim Hargrove
Women's Movement, by Maureen Ash
Women's Voting Rights, by Miles Harvey

Throughout Our History

First Ladies, by Susan Maloney Clinton
Presidential Elections, by Jim Hargrove and Miles Harvey
Smithsonian Institution, by R. Conrad Stein and Mary Collins
Supreme Court, by Kenneth Richards
White House, by Deborah Kent

American History—The Signature Series

The *Signature* books are a series about famous Americans. The books are actually named "A Story of..." and the names below. For example, "A Story of Abraham Lincoln".

Abraham Lincoln, Nina Brown Baker
Amelia Earhart, Adle de Leeuw
Andrew Jackson, Enid Lamonte Meadowcroft
Annie Oakley, Edmund Collier
Beethoven, Helen L. Kaufmann
Benjamin Franklin, Enid Lamonte Meadowcroft
Buffalo Bill, Edmund Collier

Christopher Columbus, Nina Brown Baker
Clara Barton, Olive Price
Crazy Horse, Enid Lamonte Meadowcroft
Dan Beard, Robert N. Webb
Daniel Boone, William O. Steele
Davy Crockett, Enid Lamonte Meadowcroft
Dwight D. Eisenhower, Arthur Beckharr
Edith Cavell, Iris Vinton
Eleanor Roosevelt, Lorena A. Hickok
Florence Nightingale, Margaret Leighton
Franklin D. Roosevelt, Lorena A. Hickok
General Custer, Margaret Leighton
George Washington Carver, Arna Bontemps
George Washington, Enid Lamonte Meadowcroft
Geronimo, Jim Kjelgaard
Good Queen Bess, Alida Sims Malkus
Haydn, Helen L. Kaufmann
Helen Keller, Lorena A. Hickok
Jacqueline Kennedy, Alida Sims Malkus
Joan of Arc, Jeanette C. Nolan
John J. Audubon, Joan Howard
John Paul Jones, Iris Vinton
Kit Carson, Edmund Collier
Lafayette, Hazel Wilson
Leif Ericson, William O. Steele
Louis Pasteur, Alida Sims Malkus
Louisa May Alcott, Joan Howard
Mad Anthony Wayne, Hazel Wilson
Madame Curie, Alice Thorne
Marco Polo, Olive Price
Mark Twain, Joan Howard
Martha Washington, Jeannette Covert Nolan
Mozart, Helen L. Kaufmann
Pocahontas, Shirley Grahm
President Kennedy, Iris Vinton

Robert E. Lee, Iris Vinton
Robert Louis Stevenson, Joan Howard
Stephen Foster, Esther M. Douty
Theodore Roosevelt, Winthrop Neilson
Thomas Alva Edison, Enid Lamonte Meadowcroft
Thomas Jefferson, Earl Schneck Miers
Ulysses S. Grant, Jeannette Covert Nolan
Winston Churchill, Alida Sims Malkus

American History—The "Childhood of Famous Americans" Series

This chronological list is also courtesy of "Paula's archives". Visit her website at www.PaulasArchives.com for many great book lists.

Colonial Days

James Oglethorpe, by Parks
John Alden, by Burt
John Peter Zenger, by Long
John Smith, by Barton
Myles Standish, by Stevenson
Peter Stuyvesant, by Widdemer
Phillis Wheatley, by Borland and Speicher
Pocahontas, by Seymour
Pontiac, by Peckham
Squanto, by Stevenson
Virginia Dare, by Stevenson
William Bradford, by Smith
William Penn, by Mason

Struggle for Independence

Anthony Wayne, by Stevenson
Ben Franklin, by Stevenson
Betsy Ross, by Weil
Crispus Attucks, by Millender

Can Morgan, by Bryant
Ethan Allen, by Winders
Francis Marion, by Steele
George Rogers Clark, by Wilkie
George Washington, by Stevenson
Israel Putnam, by Stevenson
John Hancock, by Cleven
John Paul Jones, by Snow
Martha Washington, by Wagoner
Molly Pitcher, by Stevenson
Nathan Hale, by Stevenson
Nathanael Greene, by Peckham
Patrick Henry, by Barton
Paul Revere, by Stevenson
Tom Jefferson, by Monsell

Early National Growth

Abigail Adams, by Wagoner
Alec Hamilton, by Higgins
Andy Jackson Stevenson
Benjamin West, by Snow
Black Hawk, by Cleven
Dan Webster, by Smith
DeWitt Clinton, by Widdemer
Dolly Madison, by Monsell
Eli Whitney, by Snow
Elias Howe, by Corcoran
Francis Scott Key, by Stevenson
Henry Clay, by Monsell
James Fenimore Cooper, by Winders
James Monroe, by Widdemer
John Audobon, by Mason
John Fitch, by Stevenson
John Jacob Astor, by Anderson
John Marshall, by Monsell

John Quincy Adams, by Weil
Lucretia Mott, by Burnett
Matthew Calbraith Perry, by Scharbach
Nancy Hanks, by Stevenson
Noah Webster, by Higgins
Oliver Hazard Perry, by Long
Osceola, by Clark
Rachel Jackson, by Govan
Robert Fulton, by Henry
Samuel Morse, by Snow
Sequoyah, by Snow
Stephen Decatur, by Smith
Stephen Foster, by Higgins
Washington Irving, by Widdemer
William H. McGuffey, by Williams
Zack Taylor, by Wilkie

Westward Movement

Brigham Young, by Jordan and Frisbee
Buffalo Bill, by Stevenson
Daniel Boone, by Stevenson
Davy Crockett, by Parks
Gail Borden, by Paradis
James J. Hill, by Comfort
Jed Smith, by Burt
Jessie Fremont, by Wagoner
Jim Bowie, by Winders
Jim Bridger, by Winders
Kit Carson, by Stevenson
Lotta Crabtree, by Place
Meriwether Lewis, by Bebenroth
Narcissa Whitman, by Warner
Sacagawea, by Seymour
Sam Houston, by Stevenson
Simon Kenton, by Wilkie

Tecumseh, by Stevenson
Will Clark, by Wilkie
William Farago, by Wilkie
William Henry Harrison, by Peckham
Zeb Pike, by Stevenson

The Nation Divided

Abe Lincoln, by Stevenson
Abner Doubleday, by Dunham
Bedford Forrest, by Parks
Clara Barton, by Stevenson
David Farragut, by Long
Harriet Beecher Stowe, by Widdemer
Jeb Stuart, by Winders
Jeff Davis, by de Grummone and Delaune
Julia Ward Howe, by Wagoner
Mary Todd Lincoln, by Wilkie
Raphael Semmes, by Snow
Robert E. Lee, by Monsell
Tom Jackson, by Monsell
U.S. Grant, by Stevenson

Reconstruction and Expansion

Aleck Bell, by Widdemer
Allan Pinkerton, by Borland and Speicher
Andrew Carnegie, by Henry
Booker T. Washington, by Stevenson
Chief Joseph, by Burt
Cyrus McCormick, by Dobler
Dorothea Dix, by Melin
Eugene Field, by Borland and Speicher
Frances Willard, by Mason
George Custer, by Stevenson
George Pullman, by Myers
Harry Houdini

Henry Wadsworth Longfellow, by Melin
Joel Chandler Harris, by Weddle
John Deere, by Bare
John Muir
John Wanamaker, by Burt
Lew Wallace, by Schaaf
Louisa Alcott, by Wagoner
Luther Burbank, by Burt
Maria Mitchell, by Melin
Mark Twain, by Mason
Mary Mapes, Dodge by Mason
P.T. Barnum, by Stevenson
Robert Todd Lincold, by Anderson
Sitting Bull, by Stevenson
Susan B. Anthony, by Monsell
Tom Edison, by Guthridge

Turn of the Century

Annie Oakley, by Wilson
Dan Beard, by Mason
Elizabeth Blackwell, by Henry
F.W. Woolworth, by Myers
George Carver, by Stevenson
George Dewey, by Long
George Eastman, by Henry
George Westinghouse, by Dunham
J. Sterling Morton, by Moore
James Whitcomb Riley, by Mitchell
Jane Addams, by Wagoner
John Borroughs, by Frisbee
John Philip Sousa, by Weil
Juliette Low, by Higgins
Kate Douglas Wiggin, by Mason
Katharine Lee Bates, by Myers
Liliuokalane, by Newman

The Ringling Brothers, by Burt
Robert Peary, by Clark
Teddy Roosevelt, by Parks
Walter Reed, by Higgins
Wilbur and Orville Wright, by Stevenson
Will and Charlie Mayo, by Hammontree

In Recent Years

Adlai Stevenson, by Ward
Albert Einstein, by Hammontree
Alvin C. York, by Weddle
Amelia Earhart, by Howe
A.P. Giannini, by Hammontree
Babe Didrikson, by de Grummond and Delaune
Babe Ruth, by Van Riper Jr.
Carl Ben Eielson, by Myers and Burnett
Cecil B. DeMille, by Myers and Burnett
Clyde Beatty, by Wilkie
Douglas MacArthur, by Long
Edward Bok, by Myers
Edward R. Murrow, by Myers and Burnett
Eleanor Roosevelt, by Weil
Ernie Pyle, by Wilson
Ethel Barrymore, by Newman
Franklin Roosevelt, by Weil
George Gershwin, by Bryant
George M. Cohan, by Winders
Glenn L. Martin, by Harley
Harvey S. Firestone, by Paradis
Helen Keller, by Wilkie
Henry Ford, by Aird and Ruddiman
Herbert Hoover, by Comfort
Jean Felix Piccard, by de Grummond and Delaune
Jim Thorpe, by Van Riper Jr.
John F. Kennedy, by Frisbee

John L. Lewis
Roberto Clemente (COFA) Knute Rockne, by Van Riper Jr.
Langston Hughes
Lee DeForest, by Dobler
Lou Gherig, by Van Riper Jr.
Martin Luther King Jr., by Millender
Neil Armstrong
Oliver Wendell Holmes Jr., by Durham
Richard Byrd, by Van Riper Jr.
Robert Frost, by Wilson
Robert Goddard, by Moore
Vilhjalmur Stefansson, by Myers and Burnett
Walt Disney, by Hammontree
Walter Chrysler, by Weddle
Will Rogers, by Van Riper Jr.
Woodrow Wilson, by Monsell

Canadian History

Canadian History—"Great Stories of Canada" Series

The *Great Stories of Canada* series is comparable to the American *Landmark* series. Children in grades five and up will enjoy these historically accurate books.

1) *The Scarlet Force: The Making of the Mounted Police*, by T. Morris Longstreth
2) *The Force Carries On: Sequel to "The Scarlet Force*," by T. Morris Longstreth
3) *Raiders of the Mohawk: The Story of Butler's Rangers*, by Orlo Miller
4) *The Nor'Westers: The Fight for the Fur Trade*, by Marjorie Wilkins Campbell
5) *The Golden Trail: The Story of the Klondike Rush*,

by Pierre Berton

6) *Buckskin Brigadier: The Story of the Alberta Field Force in 1885*, by Edward McCourt

7) *The Map-Maker: The Story of David Thompson*, by Kerry Wood

8) *Arctic Assignment: The Story of the "St. Roch,"* by Sgt. F.S. Farrar, RCMP

9) *Captain of the Discovery: The Story of Captain George Vancouver*, by Roderick Haig-Brown

10) *The Bold Heart: The Story of Father Lacombe*, by Josephine Phelan

11) *Redcoat Sailor: The Story of Sir Howard Douglas*, by R.S. Lambert

12) *Red River Adventure: The Story of the Selkirk Settlers*, by J.W. Chalmers

13) *The True North: The Story of Captain Joseph Bernier*, by T.C. Fairley & Charles E. Irael

14) *The Great Chief: Maskepetoon, Warrior of the Crees*, by Kerry Wood

15) *The Salt-Water Men: Canada's Deep-Sea Sailors*, by Joseph Schull

16) *The Rover: The Story of a Canadian Privateer*, by Thomas H. Raddall

17) *Revolt in the West: The Story of the Riel Rebellion*, by Edward McCourt

18) *Knights of the Air: Canadian Aces of World War I*, by John Norman Harris

19) *Frontenac and the Iroquois: The Fighting Governor of New France*, by Fred Swayze

20) *Man From St. Malo: The Story of Jacques Cartier*, by Robert D. Ferguson

21) *Battle for the Rock: The Story of Wolfe and Montcalm*, by Joseph Schull

22) *The Queen's Cowboy: James Macleod of the Mounties*, by Kerry Wood

23) *Fur Trader: The Story of Alexander Henry*, by Robert D. Ferguson

24) *The First Canadian: The Story of Champlain*, by C.T. Ritchie

25) *Adventurers from the Bay: Men of the Hudson's Bay Company*, by Clifford Wilson

26) *Ships of the Great Days: Canada's Navy in World War II*, by Joseph Schull

27) *Mutiny in the Bay: Henry Hudson's Last Voyage*, by R.S. Lambert

28) *Runner of the Woods: The Story of Young Radisson*, by C.T. Ritchie

29) *The Good Soldier: The Story of Isaac Brock*, by D.J. Goodspeed

30) *Tecumseh: The Story of the Shawnee Chief*, by Luella Bruce Creighton

31) *The Rowboat War: On the Great Lakes, 1812-1814*, by Fred Swayze

32) *The Ballad of D'Arcy McGee: Rebel in Exile*, by Josephine Phelan

33) *The Savage River: Seventy-One Days with Simon Fraser*, by Marjorie Wilkins Campbell

SCIENCE

Nature Study in the Charlotte Mason Tradition

A wonderful book for nature science is the *Handbook of Nature Study*, by Anna Botsford Comstock. It was written in 1911, and has been published ever since by Cornell University Press. Anna was the late professor of Nature Study at Cornell University. It is a good idea to read this book ahead of time, then take the children for a walk equipped with the Audubon Society Field Guides. Don't try to take this book out with you or to teach from the book. It was designed for teachers. Information is provided so that, as questions come up, you have the answers.

The *Handbook of Nature Study* is over two inches thick, and has no color pictures. However, it is a book that Charlotte Mason would have loved. If it seems a little over-whelming at first, remember that "informed" nature walks could begin after reading only the first twenty-two pages. From this point, simply look at the table of contents and follow the topics as desired.

Some other books that Charlotte Mason might have enjoyed are those by J. H. Fabre (there are many more good books by this author):

The Wonder Book of Plant Life
Animal Life in Field and Garden
Social Life in the Insect World
The Wonders of Instinct
The Life of the Fly
The life of the Spider
Fabre's Book of Insects
Our Humble Helpers

> *"What Fabre did was tell what he saw, in a style that would have swept Thoreau off his feet."*
>
> **Peattie**

Other good nature books to look for (though no longer in print) are:

Little Busybodies, by Jeannette Marks and Julia Moody
The Children's Life of the Bee, by Maruice Maeterlinck

The Country Diary of an Edwardian Lady, by Edith Holden is a beautiful book done in 1906 to record the countryside through the changing seasons in England. There are exceptionally beautiful paintings on every page of birds, butterflies, bees and flowers, reflecting her deep love of nature. They have been executed with a naturalist's eye for detail and the sensitivity of an artist. (This book is being republished in hard back and should be available soon.) After finding this book, I kept my eye open for anything else by or about Edith Holden, and to my amazement, I found two books:

The Edwardian Lady, The Story of Edith Holden, by Ina Taylor. Ina brings together a unique collection of photographs, paintings, an mementos of the Holden family, as well as excerpts from Edith's own lively correspondence and highlights from her country diary that tell the story of her life and the background against which she developed her talents.

The Nature Notes of an Edwardian Lady, by Edith Holden is a newly discovered predecessor to the previously mentioned work. It is similar in style, with Edith Holden's thoughts, anecdotes, and writings, interspersed with poetry and watercolor paintings of flowers, plants, birds and butterflies. There are also landscape scenes, which include hares, rabbits, squirrels, foxes and other animals that do not appear in the "Country Diary".

Science for the Classical Child

Those teaching via the Classical method could easily employ (and would probably thoroughly enjoy) all the books listed in the previous section. However, Classical instructors would probably want to add more "structure", especially for upper elementary and junior high school students. The following series is good. It is no longer in print, but can still be found in used bookstores:

Concepts and Challenges in Science (Series), originally published by Alklyn and Bacon, Inc.

Considering God's Creation: A Creative, Biblical Approach to Natural Science is a workbook plus teacher's guide set that explores science from a Christian point of view. It is geared for elementary-aged students with lots of cutting-and-pasting and hands-on activities. It can be used as a text for a particular year, or as a supplement to other science programs over several years. It can also be used with multiple-aged children.

For the high school student, there is a new series of books written with the Classical Christian method in mind. They are entitled, *Exploring Creation with...* (Biology, Physics, etc.) by Dr. Jay L. Wile. This program is published by Apologia Educational Ministries, the same group that published *Around the World in 180 Days*.

This complete science program is well suited for home-schooling, and will give your child a scientific education. This well-founded education will help him to make a reasoned defense of his Christian faith. It is a rigorous program, but the parent does not need to be a scientist to teach it. Most of the experiments can be done with house-hold supplies and do not require sophisticated equipment.

The *Exploring Creation With...* series was written by a single author, and was designed specifically for home-schools, not classrooms (although a lot of classroom teachers are buying these books). Classical schools love this program. Apologia Educational Ministries has curriculum support, so parents can get help if necessary.
Contact them by writing to:

Dr. Jay L. Wile,
Apologia Educational Ministries
808 Country Club Lane

Anderson, IN 46011.
Email: Jlwile@highschoolscience.com
Website: http://www.highschoolscience.com
Phone: (765) 649-4076
Fax: (765) 649-4076

MATH

Saxon Math is perfect for both Charlotte Mason and Classical educators. (Note: For those using *Saxon Math*, one must eventually choose between *Saxon Math 87* and *Saxon A1 One Half*. They are both for the same grade, but meant for different students. It is recommended that students who have used Saxon previously use the *Saxon A1 One Half*, while others use the *Saxon Math 87*.)

There are many other good math programs. It doesn't really matter which text or program is used, as long as children learn their basic math skills (addition, subtraction, multiplication and division) in their early years. Saxon offers a complete program, right through high school.

If students want to use a different program in high school, try *Elementary Algebra* by Harold Jacobs. It is an excellent text. (Classical schools love this book.) Follow this with *Geometry* also by Harold Jacobs

To add a little "Charlotte Mason" use *Mathematicians are People, Too*, (two volumes) by Luetta & Wilbert Reimer, and published by Dale Seymour. These are stories from the lives of great mathematicians. The stories are true stories about real people.

Also, have a look at *Family Math*. This is a book written for parents of grade K-8 children, and is meant to be used at home. *Family Math* is an enrichment program, not a complete curriculum. A knowledge of math is not assumed, and the explanations are very simple and very interesting.

Contact Lawrence Hall, Science University of California for a copy, or look for it in your local homeschool bookstore.

ENGLISH

English may be the most difficult subject in which to blend the Charlotte Mason and Classical Education approaches. Be sure to look at a variety of programs before choosing one for your child.

Charlotte Mason would have recommended Simply Grammar. (We know this because she wrote it! Karen Andreola's *Simply Grammar* is the revised and expanded version of Charlotte Mason's *First Grammar Lessons*.) Charlotte's view was that children learn grammar and writing skills best by osmosis—that is, by exposure to excellent writing and grammar through classic authors such as Charles Dickens. Charlotte believed that the more you read these authors, the better your English skills will become. Simply Grammar is intended to be used in the fourth grade, and then to be repeated a few years later. Simply Grammar is a non-consumable text. (Charlotte Mason did not believe in workbooks.)

For Classical Education, there are a few options available. Get hold of a copy of Laura Berquist's book, *Designing Your Own Classical Curriculum* and Jesse Wise and Susan Wise Bauer's book, *The Well Trained Mind*. Both are excellent resources that provide many suggestions for English curriculum. The very best programs I have found are:

Excellence in Writing, a very structured, yet adaptable program that teaches children how to write, and write well. This program is outstanding. The creator, Andrew Pudewa, also has a series of videotapes available which teach parents how to teach the program. This book is available new through the Institute for Excellence in Writing: 1-800-856-5815. It can also be purchased used through the Homeschool Potpourri bookstore (425) 820-4626, or on the web at Charlotte's Classical USED BOOKshelf: http://www.JennySockey.com

Shurley Method—English Made Easy. Homeschooling Edition—Grammar & Composition. This innovative, easy-to follow program successfully teaches students of all learning abilities through lessons that constantly expose them to "see it, hear it, say it, do it" activities. Many Classical Education schools love the original "Shurley Grammar". In response to requests from home educators across the country, the Shurley Method has just introduced this new Homeschool edition. This program is well suited to Classical Education's grammar stage. Each kit includes a CD with jingles as well as question and answer flows. It can be purchased from Shurley Instructional Materials, Inc. at 1-800-566-2966 or www.shurley.com.

There is another program worth mentioning which I have not seen recommended by either Charlotte Mason or Classical Education advocates. This program, *Understanding Writing*, by Susan Bradrick, and published by Bradrick Family Enterprises, incorporates all of English (not just writing) and runs from first to twelfth grades. (You can buy this program used from Homeschool Potpourri or from the author's online book service.) In addition, children of different ages can work at the same time. There are some other books required for this program: *The English Handbook*, by Rod and Staff Publishing, and the *Handbook of Grammar and Composition*, by A Beka are necessary as Susan refers to them both at different times throughout the program. *Easy Grammar*, by Wanda Phillips (published by ISHA Enterprises 1-800-641-6015), is used in grade seven. And *Easy Writing*, also published by ISHA, is recommended for grade 8.

It is important for parents to get a good grasp of the *Understanding Writing* program before using it with their children. It is recommended that parents read the first 36 pages, leave the book for a few days, and then re-read that section again. It will make a tremendous difference in the outcome of the program. Next, go through the checklist at the back of the book. *Understanding Writing* lists the things that children should know by the end of each grade. If there are gaps, ensure that they are filled in, because the program constantly builds on the previous year's foundation.

This program does not teach "standard" grammar in grades one to six, however, the children are learning grammar. In grade seven, children will use *Easy Grammar*. Be patient—don't teach this book before grade seven, as most are not ready for it yet. Use either the original *Easy Grammar* (a big red book) or the *Easy Grammar Plus*, which is the latest version—either are fine. The *Understanding Writing* program is scripted and explains exactly what to do and how to teach. *Understanding Writing* teaches from a Christian perspective.

SPELLING

As far as Spelling goes, I believe that the more one reads good literature the better one becomes in spelling. Charlotte Mason believed in writing a spelling word on the black board (now it's called a white board and you don't use chalk) one word at a time and tell the child to look at the word and keep looking at it until he can "see" it in his mind's eye. It may take some time until the child understands what you mean but when he does then it really does work. What is really neat about doing spelling this way is that they never forget it as long as they could "see" it in their mind. I did this in my school and I used *The Natural Speller* by Kathryn Stout, B.S.Ed., M. Ed. (published by Design-a-Study, 408 Victoria Ave. Wilmington, DE 19804). It has a good list of words to use for 1st-8th grade. Since it is all in one book you don't have to worry about grades - just work your way through the book. Other people like to use words from their writing and that is okay, too, as long as they have the child "see" it in their minds eye.

As far as the Classical Education method goes, the authors of "The Well Trained Mind" recommend a totally different system using the Modern Curriculum Press' *Spelling Workout*. There is a workbook for each grade level. If you want to go this route then still try and use the mind's eye idea. It works.

POETRY

I have over four bookshelves of poetry books, myself. Here are some of my favorites:

> *Favorite Poems Old and New*, by Helen Ferris. Available from Bob Jones University Press.
> *A Child's Garden of Verses*, by Robert Louis Stevenson.
> *American History in Verse*, by Burton Steveson. This is an old book now being published by Bob Jones University Press.
> *The Harp and Laurel Wreath, Poetry and Dictation for the Classical Curriculum*, by Laura M. Berquist, published by Ignatius. This book is beautiful and

offers wonderful insights on dictation. The poems are arranged by age level (Grammatical, Dialectical, and Rhetorical stages). Here is a quote from Mrs. Berquist on the importance of poetry:

"It is a temptation for a person who is home-schooling children to save fine arts appreciation for days when religion, English, mathematics, science, history, geography, literature, and penmanship are all finished. The problem, of course, is that all of these things seldom get done. Therefore the introduction of beautiful pictures, great music, and excellent poetry remains an activity to do `someday'.

"This is a mistake, because the appreciation of the fine arts is formative for the soul. The old adage, `You are what you eat' could be changed truthfully to say, `You are what you see and hear.' The models in one's imagination and memory become a part of the soul and effects all the rest of life.

If the soul holds good, true, beautiful, noble and heroic images, it will be inclined to love those things. Additionally, since whatever is true is also beautiful, an appreciation of the beautiful prepares the way for an appreciation of the truth. If children love the beautiful they will be disposed to love the truth, as truth, when they are older. Thus, even in terms of intellectual formation, fostering the fine arts is important."

Laura Berquist

ART

"Looking at art is one way of listening to God"

Sister Wendy Beckett

Charlotte Mason encouraged parents to get large prints of art (8 1/2 x 11 or larger). She allowed the children to look at the art for some time, then to describe what they saw after the removal of the picture. This process helps to develop the skills of observation and description. Charlotte also advocated the study of one artist for several weeks at a time, with the focus on one work of art per week. This artwork should be present for the entire week, placed strategically where the children will see it often.

A good series for this purpose is *The Great Artists: A Library of Their Lives, Times, and Paintings*. If it is not still in print, it can be found fairly easily in used bookstores and is relatively inexpensive.

"Every child seems to be an incipient artist— loving to draw with pencils, crayons, and water colors. It is important for us to encourage this desire for producing beauty—a desire innate in all of us who are made in the image and likeness of the primary artist."

Mary Lynch

Art: Books for Teaching Art

A Child's History of Art, by V. M. Hillyer & E.G. Huey. No longer being published and can be quite expensive even though it is used but well worth the money.
StoneBridge Art Guide, A Christian History Curriculum Guide for Teaching and Learning Art in the American

Christian Principle Approach. Published by StoneBridge Educational Foundation

Adventures in Art: "Understanding the Flow of Thought as Seen Through Art", Comprehensive Study Guide by David Quine. Published by The Cornerstone curriculum Project

The Annotated Mona Lisa, A crash course in art history from prehistoric to post-modern, by Carol Strickland,Ph.D.

History of Art for Young People, by H.W. Janson and Anthony F. Janson

Drawing with Children, A Creative Method for Adult Beginners, Too, by Mona Brookes. Published by G. P. Putnam's Sons

Drawing For Older Children & Teens, A Creative Method for Adult Beginners, Too, by Mona Brookes. Published by Jeremy P. Tarcher, Inc.

Drawing on the Right Side of the Brain, A Course in Enhancing Creativity and Artistic Confidence, by Betty Edwards. Published by J. P. Tarcher, Inc.

A child's Book of Art, Great Pictures, First Words, selected by Lucy Micklewait. Published by Dorling Kindersley

Looking at Pictures, An Introduction to Art for Young People, by Joy Richardson. Published by Harry N. Abrams, Inc.

A Child's Book of Prayer in Art, by Sister Wendy Beckett. Published by DK Publishing, inc.

Michelangelo Pieta Photographed, by Robert Hupka. No words can describe this, it is awesome!

The Renaissance, The Invention of Perspective-Part of the "Art for Children" Series, by Lillo Canto. Chelsea House Publishers.

Jesus of Nazareth , The Life of Christ Through Pictures, illustrated with paintings from the National Gallery of art, Washington, D.C. Simon & Schuster books for young Readers.

Sister Wendy's Story of Painting, in association with the National Gallery of Art, Washington, D.C. DK publishers.

Art: Historical Fiction & Biographies

There are some very good Historical Fiction and Biographies concerning Art. Here are some of them:

Antonio's Apprenticeship, Painting a Fresco in Renaissance Italy, written and illustrated by Taylor Morrison. Published by Holiday House.

Linnea in Monet's Garden, by Christina Bjork & Lina Anderson. Published by R&S books.

Waiting For Filippo, The Life of Renaissance Architect FIlippo Brunelleschi– A Pop-Up Book, by Michael Bender. Published by Chronicle Books

Leonardo Da Vinci, by Diane Stanley. Published by Morrow Jonior Books

Michelangelo's Surprise, by Tony Parillo. Published by Farrar Straus Giroux

Art: Books on famous artists

Famous American Painters, by Roland Mckinney. No longer being published but worth looking for in a used bookstore or library.

Great Artists of America, by Lillian Freedgood. (Out of print. Used Bookstore.)

Rembrandt, The Old Testament, by Thomas Nelson publishers.. The Bible version used in this publication is the New King James Version.

The Norman Rockwell Storybook, told by Jan Wahl.

Willie was Different, A child's story by Norman Rockwell. Also, any other books of Rockwell''s paintings, all are great.

Art: Book Series

Here are some art series that are good. Many of them are still in print:

What Makes A Raphael a Raphael? (Also, look for the same titles about the artists: *Rembrant, Van Gogh, Leonardo, Picasso, Monet, Cassatt, Goya, Degas, and Bruegel*) These are all done through the Metropolitan Museum of art. A different author describes each artist.

Getting to Know the World's Greatest Artists, series written and illustrated by Mike Venezia. The artists include Da Vinci, Botticelli, Michelangelo, Salvador Dali, Monet, and Picasso. There are also some books in this series about musical composers.

Famous Artists, An Introduction to the Artist's Life and Work. Van Gogh, Michelangelo, Cezanne, Leonardo Da Vinci

Famous Children, series by Tony Hart, illustrated by Susan Hellard. Artists include Leonardo Da Vinci, Michelangelo, Picasso, and Toulouse-Lautrec. There are also some music titles.

Art for Children, series by Ernest Rabott. A Harper Trophy book. Includes Leonardo Da Vinci, Velasquez, Henri Rousseau, Frederic Remington, Marc Chagall, Albrecht Durer, Pablo Picasso, and Henri De Toulouse-Lautrec

Masters of Art Series. All of the different artists are written about by different authors. Leonardo Da Vinci — artist, inventor & scientist of the Renaissance.

Michelangelo, master of the Italian Renaissance. Giotto and Medieval art — the lives and works of the medieval artists, Rembrandt and 17th-century Holland, the Dutch nation and its painters. The Story of Sculpture, from prehistory to the present

The Library of Great Masters Series - Duccio,Simone Martini, Masaccio, Filippo Lippi, Raphael, Canaletto, Piero Della Francesca, Benozzo Gozzoli, Correggio. Published by Scala/Riverside

The Great Artists—A library of their lives, times, and paintings. Not sure if this is still being printed, but it is fairly inexpensive used. These paperback books have very nice pictures.

1) *Van Gogh*
2) *Rembrandt*
3) *Winslow Homer*
4) *Renoir*
5) *Michelangelo*
6) *Picasso*
7) *Da Vinci*
8) *Toulouse-Lautrec*
9) *El Greco*
10) *Dagas*
11) *Titian*
12) *Modigliani*
13) *Rubens*
14) *Whistler*
15) *Raphael*
16) *Gauguin*
17) *Gainsborough*
18) *Cezanne*
19) *Vermeer*
20) *Matisse*
21) *Goya*

22) *Monet*
23) *Velzquez*
24) *Bonnard*
25) *Manet*

MUSIC

"There are things in the Christian world which cause us to be sad. One of these is that for many Christians classical music is a complete vacuum, This robs individual Christians and their children of one of the very rich areas of joy in this world."

Dr. Francis Schaeffer

Books About Music

What to Listen for in Music, by Aaron Copland—This is a classic work, the only book of it's kind written by a great composer. A Mentor Book

Raising Musical Kids, by Patrick Kavanaugh. Great ideas to help your child develop a love for music. This author also wrote *The Spiritual Lives of Great Composers*. VB Vine Books, Servant Publications.

Music of the Great Composers, by Patrick Kavanaugh, previously published as *A Taste for the Classics*. A listener's guide to the best of classical music. Zondervan Publishing House. Patrick is also listed in this section under other headings for more books. He is very knowledgeable and is also a Christian. I recommend him highly.

Music Education in the Christian Home, by Dr. Mary Ann Froehlich. How to nurture the musician in your child. Noble Publishing Associates.

How to Grow a Young Music Lover, by Cheri Fuller, Helping your child discover and enjoy the world of music. Harold Shaw Publishers

Classical Music for Dummies, by David Pogue & Scott Speck. The fun and easy way to understand and enjoy classical music. "The perfect way to go from dummy to expert" - Andre Watts, pianist IDG Books Worldwide

Music—Books by a Single Author, for Children:

In Music Land, by George P. Upton. A handbook for young people. Copyright 1913. (Out of print. Used Bookstore.) This book has many stories of the child-hoods of famous composers, the story of musical forms, the orchestra, and dictionary of terms. A fun book.

Prince Melody in Music Land, by Elizabeth Simpson. Musical fairy tales for musical children. Copyright 1917. (Out of print. Used Bookstore.)

The Little Princes of Music Land, by Elizabeth Simpson. Childhood of great composers. Copyright 1926. (Out of print. Used Bookstore.)

Music—Hymn Stories

I have long enjoyed the stories behind the hymns that are a part of my childhood. Here are the names of some books that I think that you would find interesting along with your children.

Stories Behind Popular Songs and Hymns, by Lindsay Terry. This book does not include music, only the words. Baker Book House Publisher

Famous Stories of Inspiring Hymns, by Ernest K. Emurian. Baker Book House Publisher

Living Stories of Famous Hymns, by Ernest K. Emurian. Baker Book House Publisher

A *Treasury of Hymn Stories*, by Amos R. Wells. Brief Biographies with their best Hymns. Baker Book House Publisher

101 Hymn Stories, by Kenneth W. Osbeck. Inspiring, factual backgrounds and experiences that prompted the writing of 101 favorite hymns. Kregel Publications

101 More Hymn Stories, by Kenneth W. Osbeck. Kregel Publications

52 Hymn Stories Dramatized, by Kenneth W. Osbeck. Compelling adaptations of the stories behind some of the world's favorite hymns. Kregel publications

Amazing Grace, by Kenneth W. Osbeck. 366 Inspiring hymn stories for daily devotions. Kregel publications.

Learning History and Culture through Music

America 1750-1890: The Heart of a New Land, written by Diana Waring. History alive through music. Hear & Learn Publications

Westward Ho! The Heart of the Old West, written by Diana Waring. History alive through music. Hear & Learn Publications

Musical Memories of Laura Ingalls Wilder, written & edited by William T. Anderson. History alive through music. Hear & Learn Publications

Civil War Songs, with historical narration by Keith & Rusty McNeil WEM records

Colonial and Revolution Songs, with historical narration by Keith & Rusty McNeil WEM records

History Sings, by Hazel Gertrude Kinscella, Backgrounds of American music. Copyright 1948 (Out of print. Used Bookstore.)

America Sings, by Carl Carmer, Stories and songs of our country's growing. Copyright 1942. (Out of print. Used Bookstore.)

Stories of Our American Patriotic Songs, by Dr. John Henry Lyons, including words and music copyright 1940. (Out of print. Used Bookstore.)

Cowboy Jamboree: Western Songs & Lore, by Harold W. Felton Copyright 1951. (Out of print. Used Bookstore.)

Music—Coloring Books

I really enjoy using quality coloring books to enhance learning. I use them either while I am reading to them, or after, for those children who cannot listen and do something else at the same time.

Color the Classics—Godly Composers: Antonio Vivaldi, Johann Sebastian Bach, George Frideric Handel, and Franz Josef Haydn by Carmen Ziarkowski. Produced by Color the Classics. Biographical coloring book and cassette tape set.

Color the Classics—Hymn Writers, Vol. 2: Martin Luther (1483-1546), Isaac Watts (1674-1748), Charles Wesley (1707-1788), John Newton (1725-1807), and Fanny Crosby (1820-1915) by Carmen Ziarkowski. Produced by Color the Classics

Color the Christmas Classics. Carols that honor Christ. Produced by Color the Classics

Bellerophon produces the following coloring books:
American Composers
Composers
Early Composers

Great Composers—Bach to Berlioz
Great Composers—Chopin to Tchaikovsky
Great composers—Mahler to Stravinsky

Music—Biographies, Multiple Composers

These books are recommended for older children with a high reading level:

Milton Cross Encyclopedia of the Great Composers and Their Music, by Milton Cross and David Ewen. Copyright 1953. May still be in print. Two-volume set.

The Lives of the Great Composers, by Harold C. Schonberg. W.W. Norton & Co., Inc.

Lives of the Musicians—Good Times, Bad Times (And What the Neighbors Thought), written by Kathleen Krull. Book and tapes (2) set. Harcourt Brace & Co.

Famous Composers for Young People, by Gladys Burch & John Wolcott. Copyright 1939. (Out of print. Used Bookstore.)

Portraits of the World's Best-Known Musicians, by Guy McCoy. Copyright 1943. (Out of print. Used Bookstore.)

Story Lives of American Composers, by Katherine Little Bakeless. Copyright 1941. (Out of print. Used Bookstore.)

American Composers of Our Time, by Joseph Machlis. Some more contemporary composers. Copyright 1963. (Out of print. Used Bookstore.)

History's 100 Greatest Composers, by Helen L. Kaufmann. Copyright 1957. (Out of print. Used Bookstore.)

Minute Sketches of Great Composers, by Hansl and Kaufmann. Copyright 1932. (Out of print. Used Bookstore.)

The Gift of Music, Great Composers and Their Influence, by Jane Stuart Smith and Betty Carlson. Crossway Books.

Spiritual Lives of the Great Composers, by Patrick kavanaugh. An inspiring chronicle of classical music's Christian heritage. Zondervan Publishing House.

Music—Individual Biographies

America, I Hear You, by Barbara Mitchell. A story about George Gershwin. (Out of print. Used Bookstore.)

The Story of George Gershwin, by David Ewen. (Out of print. Used Bookstore.)

Mozart, by Manuel Komroff. (Out of print. Used Bookstore.)

The Mozart Handbook, compiled and edited by Louis Biancolli. A guide to the man and his music. (Out of print. Used Bookstore.)

Young Mozart, by Rachel Isadora. Published by Viking

Bach's Big Adventure, by Sallie Ketcham. Published by Orchard Books

Sebastian, A Book About Bach, by Jeanette Winter. Browndeer Press, Harcourt Brace & Co.

Johann Strauss, Father and Son, by H. E. Jacob. (Out of print. Used Bookstore.)

Stormy Victory, The Story of Tchaikovsky, by Claire Lee Purdy. (Out of print. Used Bookstore.)

Aaron Copland His Life, by Catherine Owens Peare. (Out of print. Used Bookstore.)

Scott Joplin and the Ragtime Years, by Mark Evans. (Out of print. Used Bookstore.)

Song of the Waterfall, by Elisabeth Kyle, the story of Edward & Nina

Grieg. (Out of print. Used Bookstore.)

Making Music: Leonard Bernstein, by Shirley Bernstein. (Out of print. Used Bookstore.)

Clara Schumann, Piano Virtuoso, by Susanna Reich. Clarion books

Stephen Foster, Boy Minstrel, by Helen Boyd Higgins. Part of *The Childhood of Famous Americans* series. (Out of print. Used Bookstore.)

Music—Sets of Individual Biographies

Sets, or a series on individual composers.

Mozart, Young Music Genius, by Louis Sabin. Troll Associates

Ludwig Van Beethoven, Young Composer, by Louis Sabin. Troll Associates

Famous Children Series, by Ann Rachlin. Barron's Publishers. Bach, Beethoven, Brahms, Chopin, Handel, Haydn, Mozart, Schuber, Schumann, Tchaikovsky

Getting to Know the World's Greatest Composers Series, written and illustrated by Mike Venezia. Published by Children's Press. Peter Tchaikovsky, George Gershwin, Aaron Copland, Ludwig Van Beethoven, Wolfgang Amadeus Mozart, George Handel, Igor Stravinsky, & Duke Ellington

Masters of Music Series. Barron's Publishers. *Beethoven and the Classical Age*, by Andrea Bergamini. *Mozart and Classical Music*, by Francesco Salvi. *Bach and Baroque Music*, by Stefano Catucci

Signature Books Series. Look for these in used bookstores. *The Story of Stephen Foster*, by Esther M. Douty. *The Story of Haydn*, by Helen L. Kaufmann. *The Story of Beethoven*, by Helen L. Kaufmann. *The Story of Mozart*, by Helen L. Kaufmann

Books authored by Madeleine B. Goss. (Out of print. Used Bookstore.)

> *Deep-Flowing Brook, The Story of Johann Sebastian Back*
>
> *Unfinished Symphony, The Story of Franz Schubert*
>
> *Beethoven: Master Musician*

Hayden & Beethoven, by Reba Paeff Mirsky. (Out of print. Used Bookstore.)

Authored by Opal Wheeler. (Out of print. Used Bookstore.)

> *Stephen Foster and His Little Dog Tray*
> *Peter Tschaikowsky and the Nutcracker Ballet*
> *Frederic Chopin, Son of Poland, Early Years*
> *Ludwig Beethoven and the Chiming Tower Bells*
> *Paganini, Master of Strings*
> *Pinafore (An operetta)*

Biographies written by Opal Wheeler and Sybil Deucher.

> *Franz Schubert and His Merry Friends*
> *Edward MacDowell and His Cabin in the Pines*
> *Mozart the Wonder Boy*
> *Joseph Hayden, the Merry Little Peasant*
> *Sebastian Back, The Boy from Thuringia*
> *Handel at the Court of Kings*

The Young Brahms, by Sybil Deucher.

Music—Classical Kids Series

These come in tapes and CDs. Some come with a book.

Mozart's Magnificent Voyage
Mozart's Magic Fantasy, A Journey Through The Magic Flute
Mr. Bach Comes to Call
Beethoven Lives Upstairs. Book also available
Vivaldi's Ring of Mystery
Tchaikovsky Discovers America. Book also available
Hallelujah Handel

Music—The Music Masters Series

These tapes and CDs feature music and significant events from each composer's life.

Vivaldi, 1675-1741 & Corelli, 1653-1713
Bach, 1685-1750
Handel, 1685-1759
Hayden, 1732-1809
Mozart, 1756-1791
Beethoven, 1770-1827
Schubert, 1797-1828
Berlioz, 1803-1869
Mendelssohn, 1809-1847
Schuman, 1810-1856 & Grieg, 1843-1907
Chopin, 1810-1849
Verdi, 1813-1901
Wagner, 1813-1883
Strauss, 1825-1899
Foster, 1826-1901 & Sousa, 1845- 1932
Brahms, 1833- 1897
Tchaikovsky, 1840-1893
Dvorak, 1841-1904

Music—Ballet

The Illustrated Book of Ballet Stories, by Barbara Newman. DK publishers

Shoes of Satin, Ribbons of Silk: Tales from the Ballet, by Antonia Barber-Kingfisher

Magic Slipper: Stories from the Ballet, by Gilda Berger. Doubleday Books

101 Stories of the Great Ballets: Scene-By-Scene Stories of the Most

Popular Ballets, Old and New, by George Balanchine & Francis Mason. Published by Doubleday.

The Parent's Book of Ballet: Answers to Critical Questions About the Care and Development of the Young Dancer, by Angela Whitehill and William Noble. Meriwether publishers

Ballet Steps: Practice to Performance, by Antony Dufort. Clarkson N. Potter Publishers

Ballet & Dance: An Usborne Guide, by Annable Thomas

Ballet, An Usborne Guide, by Annable Thomas

On Their Toes, A Russian Ballet School, by Ann Morris. Atheneum Publishers

Music—Coloring Books, Ballet

Ballet: A fact-filled Coloring Book, by Trudy Garfunkel. Part of the *Start Exploring* series.

The Story of The Nutcracker—Coloring Book, by Dover

The Nutcracker, adapted by Carin Dewhirst. This Illustrated book and full length CD present one of the world's most beloved Christmas traditions. Peter Tchaikovskt's evocative ballet weaves its spell and carries you and your child off to the magical land of the nutcracker.

Music—Symphony

The Symphony Orchestra and What it Plays, by Dorothy Berliner Commins. Part of the *All About Books* series. (Out of print. Used Bookstore.)

The Symphony: A Listener's Guide, by Michael Steinberg. Best used after the above book, for older children. Oxford University Press

Strike Up the Orchestra: A Child's Guide to Classical Music, by Carin and Joan Elizabeth Dewhirst. Part of the *Life, Times, & Music* series. Friedman/Fairfax Publishers. Book and tape set.

Peter and the Wolf, adapted by Carin and Joan Dewhirst. Book and CD set.

Music—Opera

Operas Every Child Should Know, edited by Dolores Bacon. Descriptions of the text and music of the most famous masterpieces. Copyright 1911. (Out of print. Used Bookstore.)

Stories of Wagner Operas for Children, by Elizabeth M. Wheelock copyright 1907. (Out of print. Used Bookstore.)

Sing Me a Story, by Jane Rosenberg with Introduction by Luciano

Pavarotti. The Metropolian Opera's Book of Opera Stories for Children. Thames & Hudson

Here are some books authored by Clyde Robert Bulla. This author is well known for his historical fiction for children, as well as his love of opera.

Stories of Favorite Operas, by Clyde Robert Bulla. Mr. Bulla is a skilled spinner of words. He has presented in this book 23 stories on which the musical dramas are based, a must read. (Out of print. Used Bookstore.)
More Stories of Favorite Operas.
The Ring and the Fire, stories from Wagner's Nibelung operas
Stories of Gilbert and Sullivan Operas

CHARACTER DEVELOPMENT

There are a number of excellent books by William J. Bennett:

Our Sacred Honor
Our County's Founders: A Book of Advice for Young People
The Book of Virtues
The Book of Virtues for Young People
The Children's Book of Virtues
The Children's Book of America
The Children's Book of Heroes
The De-valuing of America
The Moral Compass
The Spirit of America

For a Classical approach, try:

Introducing Christian Virtues using Aesop's Fables, by Maggie Rayner (Layout of this book). This is a quick and simple program for elementary-aged children using Aesop's Fables, scripture, and multiple-choice questions. Maggie can be contacted at her website: www.mypage.uniserve.com/~mrrayner or email: mrrayner@uniserve.com.

Charlotte Mason would have agreed with the use of Aesop's Fables to teach moral values, but would probably have preferred to have children re-tell the fables rather than use the workbook-style questions.

LATIN

"I will say at once, quite firmly, that the best grounding for education is the Latin grammar. I say this, not because Latin is traditional and medieval, but simply because even a rudimentary knowledge of Latin cuts down the labor and pains of learning almost any other subject by at least 50 per cent. It is the key to the vocabulary and structure of all the Romance languages and to the structure of all the Teutonic languages, as well as to the technical vocabulary of all the sciences and to the literature of the entire Mediterranean civilization, together with all its historical documents.

"Latin should be begun as early as possible at a time when inflected speech seems no more astonishing than any other phenomenon in an astonishing world; and when the chanting of `amo, amas, amat' is as ritually agreeable to the feelings as the chanting of `eeny, meeny, miney, mo.'"

Dorothy L. Sayers, *The Lost Tools of Learning*

"Latin was widely taught even in American high schools as late as the 1940's. It was considered necessary to the fundamental understanding of English, the history and writings of Western Civilization, and the understanding of Romance languages.

"Learning the grammar of Latin reinforces the student's understanding of the reasons for, and the use of, the parts of speech being taught in our traditional English classwork (e.g., plurals, nouns, verbs, prepositions, direct objects, tenses, etc.)."

Foundations Academy, *Understanding the Classical and Christian Difference*— A Parent's Primer

Latin is considered to be more important to the Classical method of homeschooling than to the Charlotte Mason method. However, Charlotte did teach Latin, and in fact, taught French and German at the same time. The most common argument for the continued teaching of Latin is that it is the basis of all the "romantic" languages, and makes even the learning of English easier.

For a great, simple introduction to Latin, there are a couple of card games available called *Rummy Roots*, and *More Roots*. These games explore Greek and Latin roots of English words in a fun and easy way.

English From the Roots Up is an simple book. It explores the roots of words (by Lundquist, published by Literacy Unlimited, Bellevue, Washington). This is neither a workbook nor a text. It simply provides material for memorization and games, according to the desire of the educator. It is commonly used like a vocabulary book; children are given words to learn and commit to memory over the course of a week or more.

When the children are ready for a Latin program, check out your local homeschool store or wait for the exhibitors at your next homeschool convention. There are a number of Latin programs available, some more difficult than others. One that is Christian-based is Latina Christina, by Cheryl Lowe. It is published by Memoria Press.

Latin should be started in about third grade. It is easier for a young child to pick up a new language than it is for someone older. However, young children should probably be reading and writing English fairly well prior to learning a second language.

LOGIC

"The classical emphasis on language study was brought to the New World by the Puritan colonists, who determined that every child be able to read the Bible, and every pastor be a scholar of Latin and Greek (grammar), able to determine truth from error in their doctrine (dialectic), and able to eloquently expound on the Scriptures (rhetoric). Thus the training in the trivium, under-pinned by a Biblical worldview, remained the standard of academic excellence.

"The classical concept of the trivium in education survived as the sole educational model for two millenia because it worked — it consistently produced educated men, given to `the pursuit of knowledge and the exercise of the mind in the cause of judgment.'"

Encyclopedia Brittanica
on the History of Education

Formal Logic training should begin in grade seven or eight. Here are some ideas for teaching Logic:

Critical Thinking, by Anita Harnadek, books 1 & 2, published by Midwest Publications Company, Inc.

Introductory Logic, by Douglas Wilson. Published by Canon Press, and

Intermediate Logic, by James B. Nance, also published by Canon Press. (Both of these books have training videos available.)

Traditional Logic, An Introduction to Formal Logic, by Martin Cothran, books 1 & 2, published by Memoria Press. These cover advanced Logic.

Logic, The Right Use of Reason in the Inquiry After Truth, by Isaac Watts. This was "the" textbook on clear thinking for over 200 years at both Oxford and Cambridge, as well as in New England.

Logic, by Gordon Clark, is a much sought-after Logic text. There is a workbook available for this book. Both are published by Trinity Foundation.

Better Thinking & Reasoning, Providing a Biblical Approach to the Principles of Logic, published by Bob Jones University Press.

RHETORIC

"For we let our young men and women go out unarmed, in a day when armor was never so necessary. By teaching them to read, we have left them at the mercy of the printed word. By the invention of the film and the radio, we have made certain that no aversion to reading shall secure them from the incessant battery of words, words, words. They do not know what the words mean;

they do not know how to ward them off or blunt their edge or fling them back; they are a prey to words in their emotions instead of being the masters of them in their intellects."

Dorothy L. Sayers, *The Lost Tools of Learning*

Aristotle: The Art of Rhetoric, translated by John Henry Freese, Cambridge, MA. Harvard University Press (1975)

Ciccero (Pseudo) ad Herennium, translated by Harry Caplan, Cambridge, MA. Harvard University Press (1981)

Classical Rhetoric for the Modern Student, by Edward P. J. Corbett, 4th Edition, Oxford. Oxford University Press (1998)

A Rulebook for Arguments, 2nd Edition, Indianapolois, IND. Kackett (1992)

Most of these books can be ordered from Greenleaf Press.

The authors of *A Well Trained Mind* also recommend contacting HSLDA (the Home School Legal Defense Association), a national home-education advocacy group. The HSLDA sponsors a national debate tournament for homeschoolers every year. For information, visit their website at http://www.hslda.org or write to them at P.O. Box 3000, Purcellville, VA 20134, or call them a t (540) 338-5600.

HSLDA is Republican and Christian in orientation, which some may find objectionable. The debate tounament, though, is judged on skill, not by a sectarian or political agenda.

HOW TO CHOOSE GOOD BOOKS

A Family Program for Reading Aloud, Developed by Rosalie June Slater, Foundation for American Christian Education

How to Stock a Home Library Inexpensively, by Jane A. Williams. Bluestocking Press

The Christian Literature Program, A Guide for Teaching Literature in the Home School. Heritage School House Publishing

HOW AND WHY TO READ A "GOOD BOOK"

A Landscape With Dragons, by Michael D. O'Brien. Ignatius Publishing. (Highly recommended!)

A Passion for Books, edited by Dale Salwak. St. Martin's Press

A Passion for Books, by Terry W. Glaspey. (For book lovers! This is the perfect book is for every person who loves books, and feels, as Erasmus said, "When I get a little money, I buy books; and if any is left, I buy food and clothes.")

Brightest Heaven of Invention, A Christian Guide to Six Shakespeare Plays, by Peter J. Leithart

Evaluating Books, What Would Thomas Jefferson Think About This? By Richard J. Maybury. Bluestocking Press

Heroes of the City of Man, A Christian Guide to Select Ancient Literature, by Peter J. Leithart. Canon Press

How to Read a Book, The Classic Guide to Intelligent Reading, by Mortimer J. Adler & Charles Van Doren

How to Read Slowly, Reading for Comprehension, by James W. Sire. Harold Shaw Publishers

Literature Through the Eyes of Faith, by Susan V. Gallagher & Roger Lundin. Harper Collins Publishing

Literature Under the Microscope, A Christian Case for Reading, by Louis Whitworth. Probe Ministries International

Reading Between the Lines, A Christian Guide to Literature, by Gene Edward Veith, Jr.

Reading With Deeper Eyes, The Love of Literature & The Life of Faith, by William H. Willimon. Upper Room Books

Realms of Gold, The Classics in Christian Perspective, by Leland Ryken. Harold Shaw Publishers

The Greenleaf Guide to Ancient Literature, by Cyndy Shearer. Greenleaf Press

BOOKS LISTS
Books With Book Lists

Some of these books may be out of print. If so, you may be able to find them in a used-book store.

A Child's Delight, Essays on Children's Classics, by Noel Perrin. University Press of New England

A Guide to the Great Books, by Wesley Callihan. Veritas Press

A New Look at Children's Literature, by Anderson & Groffwadsworth Publishing Co.

America as Story, Historical Fiction for Secondary Schools, by Elizabeth F. Howard. American Library Association

American Historical Fiction and Biography, by Jeanette Hotchkiss. Scarecrow Press Inc.

Babies Need Books, by Dorothy Butler. Atheneum Publishing

Books Children Love, A Guide to the Best Children's Literature, by Elizabeth Wilson. Crossway Books.

Books for Christian Students, by Bob Jones University Press

Books that Build Character, by William Kilpatrick & Gregory and Suzanne M. Wolfe. Simon & Schuster

Books to Build On, A Grade-By-Grade Resource Guide for Parents & Teachers, edited by John Holdren & E.D Hirsch, Jr. Delta Publishing

Children's Books in England & America in the 17th Century, A history and a checklist, together with the *Young Christian's Library*, the first printed catalogue of books for children, by William Sloane. King's Crown Press. (1955)

Eyeopeners! How to Choose and Use Children's Books About Real People, Places, and Things, by Beverly Kobrin. Penguin Books

Fifty Years of Children's Books, 1910—1960: Trends, Backgrounds, Influences, by Dora V. Smith. National Council of Teachers of English (1963)

Great Books of the Christian Tradition, & Other Books Which Have Shaped Our World, by Terry W. Glaspey. Harvest House Publishers

Honey For a Child's Heart, by Gladys Hunt. Zondervan Publishing House

In Review, Living Books Past & Present: A Journal on Books for Family Reading, by Bethlehem Books. (A really good quarterly publication.)

Invitation to the Classics, A Guide to Books You've always Wanted to Read, edited by Louise Cowan & O.S. Guinness. Baker Books

Landscape With Dragons, The Battle For Your Child's Mind, by Michael D. O'Brien. Ignatius Publishing (This book is a MUST READ!)

Let the Authors Speak, A Guide to Worthy Books Based on Historical Setting, by Carolyn Hatcher. Published by Old Pinnacle Publishing

Magic Kingdoms, Discovering the Joys of Childhood Classics With Your Child, by Regina Higgins. Simon & Schuster Publishing

Read For Your Life, Turning Teens Into Readers, by Gladys Hunt and Barbara Hampton. Zondervan Publishing House

The New Read-Aloud Handbook, including a giant treasury of great read-aloud books, by Jim Trelease. Penguin Books

Tending the Heart of Virtue, How Classic Stories Awaken a Child's Moral Imagination, by Vigen Guroian. Oxford University Press

The Republic of Childhood, A Critical Guide to Canadian Children's Literature in English, by Sheila Egoff. Oxford University Press

The Collector's Book of Children's Books, by Eric Quayle. Clarkson N. Potter, Inc. (1971)

Turning Back the Pages of Time, A Guide to American History through Literature, compiled by Kathy Keller. Pilgrim Enterprises (414) 785-8052. Some of the titles in this book are only found here, and they are great finds!

Note: Bethlehem books will be announcing a new book next year, tentatively called, The Stacks. This will be an annotated historical fiction resource with good family reading.

Websites With Book Lists

Nancy Keane's Booktalks:

http://nancykeane.com/booktalks/

This site is excellent. Search for books by title, subject, author, interest and age level, and much more. The book descriptions are quite thorough, and provide the publishing information.

1000 Good Books List:

http://www.classicalhomeschooling.org/celoop/1000.html

This is a Classical Education website. The "1000 Good Books" is a list compiled by 25 homeschoolers. Worth a visit.

Charlotte's Classical USED BOOKshelf

http://www.JennySockey.com

Operated by the author of this book, this site provides book lists, information, and has a large selection of used Charlotte Mason and the Classical Education books for sale.

Contact Jenny at cmandce@JennySockey.com.

Valerie's Living Books

For those looking for Living Books, try this great site:

http://www.valerieslivingbooks.com/

Paula's Archives

Another good site: www.PaulasArchives.com.

AUDIO CASSETTES

Some children enjoy learning audibly. These tapes have jingles that will help children to memorize facts, learn about the world around them, or understand math facts.

> *The Song of America's Freedoms*. This tape comes with a copy of the Constitution. Songs include the Preamble Song, What is the Constitution?, The Song of America's Freedoms, A Founding Father Speaks, A Challenge for U.S., and America. This is a great tape and the music is good, too. It is produced by International Learning Systems of North America, the same group that did the "Sing, Spell, Read and Write" phonics program. Their number is 1-800-321-8322.
>
> *The Song of the U.S. Presidents*, also by International Learning Systems of North America: 1-800-321-8322.
>
> *Take Your Hat Off When the Flag Goes By!* A Child's Musical Introduction to the Constitution. The tape comes with a coloring book. Nice music and pictures to color. Call (206) 228-4267.
>
> Audio Memory Publishers make a lot of really good tapes. Tapes are available for grammar (*Grammar Songs*) and math (*Addition*, *Subtraction*, *Multiplication* and *Division*). The math tapes come with charts and are tastefully done. Contact Audio Memory Publishers at 1-800-365-SING. Here are some more of their tapes:
>> *States Songs*
>> *Capitals*
>> *Geography Songs*

Here are some good skip counting tapes:

Skip Count Kid's Bible Heroes (305) 255-1698

One Hundred Sheep, Skip Counting Songs from the Gospels (includes songbook) (904) 475-5757

Skip Counting Songs with Mack the Muskrat. Also includes a songbook done by Math-U-See. 1-800-383-9585.

Ballads of American History, by Fred Cooper with musical accompaniment by Gregg Harris. This book includes a compact disc. Children (aged seven and up) will delight in this history set to music. 1-800-225-5259.

Twin Sisters Productions makes several tapes on a variety of subjects.

For science, there is Lyrical Life Science, a singing science text which helps children to understand the concepts of life science using traditional, patriotic and camp tunes of long ago.

Volume I—Have Fun Learning About Life Science by Singing It!

Volume II—Mammals, Ecology, and Biomes.

Volume III—The Human Body

These volumes are also available on CD and include a songbook and a workbook.

AUTHOR'S RESOURCES

Charlotte's Classical USED BOOKshelf

Jenny Sockey continues to operate a used book service via her website. She specializes in books pertaining to the Charlotte Mason and the Classical Education methods.

Jenny travels throughout the country searching for classics, out-of-print books, and even textbooks if they are recommended by a Charlotte Mason or Classical Education author. This is a great way to locate inexpensive copies of some truly wonderful books. If you are searching for a particular book, visit Jenny's website at http://www.JennySockey.com and check the listings, or send her an email to see if she can locate a copy for you. Check back often, as the inventory is constantly changing.

Jenny Sockey is available for homeschooling consultations, and is working toward re-opening her "homeschool" in Kirkland, WA. Jenny is also available for conferences and workshops. Please feel free to call her at (425) 822-0750 or contact her at cmandce@JennySockey.com.

The Homeschool Potpourri Used & New Bookstore

The Homeschool Potpourri bookstore, pioneered by Jenny Sockey, is now owned by Jenny's daughter, Colleen Aukland, and her husband, Todd Aukland. Homeschool Potpourri carries both used and new books, and has a huge number of used books in stock. If you don't see the book you want on Jenny's website, contact Todd or Colleen at the bookstore: (425) 820-4626, or visit their website at www.homeschoolpotpourri.com.